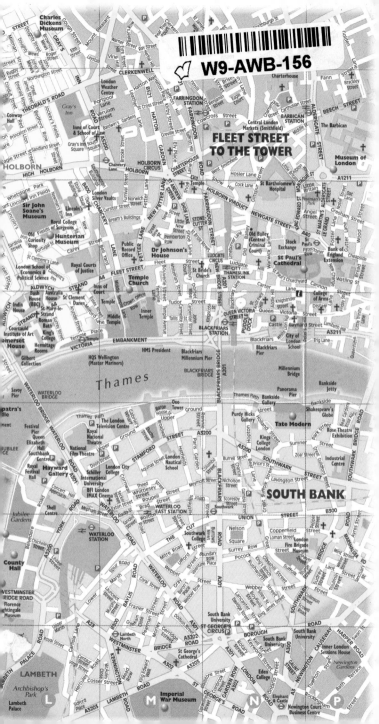

Fodor's

London's
25Best

by Louise Nicholson

Fodor's Travel Publications
New York • Toronto •
London • Sydney • Auckland
www.fodors.com

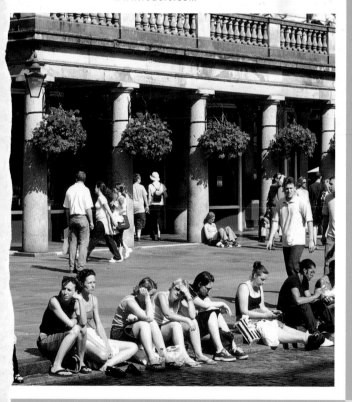

How to Use
This Book

KEY TO SYMBOLS

✚ Map reference to the accompanying fold-out map

✉ Address

☎ Telephone number

🕐 Opening/closing times

🍴 Restaurant or café

🚆 Nearest rail station

Ⓜ Nearest Tube (Metro) station

🚌 Nearest bus route

⛴ Nearest riverboat or ferry stop

♿ Facilities for visitors with disabilities

❓ Other practical information

▷ Further information

ℹ Tourist information

✋ Admission charges: Expensive (over £10), Moderate (£5–£10), and Inexpensive (£5 or less)

★ Major Sight   ★ Minor Sight

👣 Walks   🚌 Excursions

🎁 Shops

🎭 Entertainment and Nightlife

🍴 Restaurants

This guide is divided into four sections

• Essential London: An introduction to the city and tips on making the most of your stay.

• London by Area: We've broken the city into six areas, and recommended the best sights, shops, entertainment venues, nightlife and restaurants in each one. Suggested walks help you to explore on foot.

• Where to Stay: The best hotels, whether you're looking for luxury, budget or something in between.

• Need to Know: The info you need to make your trip run smoothly, including getting about by public transport, weather tips, emergency phone numbers and useful websites.

Navigation In the London by Area chapter, we've given each area its own colour, which is also used on the locator maps throughout the book and the map on the inside front cover.

Maps The fold-out map accompanying this book is a comprehensive street plan of London. The grid on this fold-out map is the same as the grid on the locator maps within the book. We've given grid references within the book for each sight and listing.

Contents

ESSENTIAL LONDON	4–18
Introducing London	4–5
A Short Stay in London	6–7
Top 25	8–9
Shopping	10–11
Shopping by Theme	12
London by Night	13
Eating Out	14
Restaurants by Cuisine	15
If You Like...	16–18

LONDON BY AREA	19–106
SOUTH BANK	**20–32**
Area Map	22–23
Sights	24–28
Walk	29
Entertainment and Nightlife	31
Restaurants	32

FLEET STREET TO THE TOWER	33–44
Area Map	34–35
Sights	36–41
Walk	42
Shopping	43
Entertainment and Nightlife	43
Restaurants	44

COVENT GARDEN TO BLOOMSBURY	45–58
Area Map	46–47
Sights	48–53
Shopping	54–55
Entertainment and Nightlife	56
Restaurants	57–58

WESTMINSTER AND ST. JAMES'S	59–80
Area Map	60–61
Sights	62–75
Walk	76
Shopping	77
Entertainment and Nightlife	79
Restaurants	80

AROUND HYDE PARK	81–92
Area Map	82–83
Sights	84–89
Shopping	90
Entertainment and Nightlife	91
Restaurants	92

FARTHER AFIELD	93–106
Area Map	94–95
Sights	96–102
Walk	103
Shopping	104
Entertainment and Nightlife	105
Restaurants	106

WHERE TO STAY	107–112
Introduction	108
Budget Hotels	109
Mid-Range Hotels	110–111
Luxury Hotels	112

NEED TO KNOW	113–125
Planning Ahead	114–115
Getting There	116–117
Getting Around	118–119
Essential Facts	120–123
Timeline	124–125

Introducing London

Prepare for London to challenge your expectations. The dynamic British capital's traditions, from Savile Row outfitters to parading Horse Guards, thrive alongside a cutting-edge cultural calendar, revived arts venues and museums, and world-class restaurants.

Whole areas of the capital have been revitalized. A redundant power station is now home to Tate Modern, and St. Paul's cathedral has been cleaned to reveal its beautiful grey stone. The Jubilee underground line and the Thames's new Millennium Bridge make visiting much easier. These have been catalysts for the revival of London from Docklands right along to Westminster, and especially on the South Bank, which is once more part of mainstream London. Meanwhile, massive redevelopments are coming to fruition in the areas of Paddington and King's Cross. And for the 2012 Olympic Games, the far east end of London will be transformed and revitalized.

Amid all this change, the greatness of London's 2,000 years of history has not been quashed. Visitors can still roam around one of Britain's finest medieval forts, the Tower of London, or visit a real royal home, Buckingham Palace. Equally, they can picnic in one of the parks or take a boat ride along the Thames to evoke times when this was the backbone of London and its great port.

Londoners themselves—while appreciating their good-value theatre, free museums, great buildings and comforting traditions—are likely to moan about just about everything else, from the horrendously high cost of property and living to the local taxes and the withdrawal of the famous Routemaster red bus. Yet, in truth, they know they are living in the world's greatest and most vibrant city. London, the political, financial and artistic capital of Britain, is hard to beat. Everything you could ever want is here; it is up to you to take it and enjoy it.

Facts + Figures

- With a population of 7.5 million, London is Europe's largest city.
- Greater London covers 1,584sq km (618sq miles).
- There are 150 theatres, 3,800 pubs, 233 nightclubs, 40,000 shops, 21,000 registered taxis, 6,000 restaurants.

LONDON'S BOSS

With the establishment of the Greater London Authority in 1999, Londoners voted for their first Mayor of all London, Ken Livingstone. He kept his pledge to improve public transportation and the environment. In May 2008, Mr Livingstone was ousted from his post by Boris Johnson, bringing his own agenda of proposals for the city.

LOCATION, LOCATION

The London Monopoly board game, where players' aim is to become property tycoons, neatly reflected property values for decades. Now the city's revitalization and consequent changes in real estate fashion have inspired a 70th birthday Monopoly edition that drops such gems as Old Kent Road in preference of the more trendy Soho and King's Road.

BEATING THE COSTS

London is expensive. So, start by working out what is free. Top of the list are most major museums and galleries, the parks, monuments such as churches, and a variety of entertainment such as music. To cut unavoidable costs, buy a Travel Pass and perhaps the London Sightseeing Pass (www.londonpass.com).

A Short Stay in London

DAY 1

Morning Take the Tube down to Westminster; great views of the **Houses of Parliament** (▷ 65) and central London from Westminster Bridge. Then, spot the statues to see who's who in Britain as you walk around Parliament Square, then up Whitehall to Trafalgar Square.

Mid-morning Visit 'tkts' in nearby Leicester Square (opens 10am Mon–Sat, 12 on Sun) to buy your reduced price theatre tickets for that night. Then visit the **National Gallery** (▷ 66). Use the computers to print out your ideal tour—do not miss the restored main entrance lobby or the Renaissance pics in the Sainsbury Wing. Excellent museum shopping, too.

Lunch Stop here at the National Gallery's café, or splurge out round the corner at the rooftop restaurant of the **National Portrait Gallery** (▷ 67); great food and views (well worth booking ahead).

Mid-afternoon Walk through **Covent Garden** (▷ 52), enjoying the market stalls, the street entertainment—and perhaps pause at **Paul** (▷ 58) the patisserie on Bedford Street.

Dinner Two options: eat pretheatre here in Covent Garden, perhaps at **Lowlander** (▷ 57) on Drury Lane, a gastropub known for its beers and wines and for its all-day food that includes a delicious risotto. Or be a true Londoner and eat after the show near your theatre.

Evening Leave plenty of time to reach your theatre. Avoid intermission lines by ordering your drinks before curtain up. If you are intending to eat afterwards, seek out your restaurant before the show and make a booking.

DAY 2

Morning If the day is dry and sunny, start with breakfast at **Inn the Park** (▷ 80, opens 8am Mon–Fri, 9am Sat, Sun) in **St. James's Park** (▷ 68), then explore this magical royal park while the dew is still on the undulating lawns. From the bridge over the lake there are wonderful views of **Buckingham Palace** (▷ 62) and the soaring spires of Westminster Palace.

Mid-morning If you want to go to a show tonight, go to 'tkts' in Leicester Square (▷ Day 1, opposite); then take a bus along Piccadilly to Hyde Park Corner; otherwise, walk up the Mall and through Green Park. Take a ramble through **Hyde Park** (▷ 89) to **Kensington Gardens** (▷ 84), checking out the roses, the Round Pond and dog-walking Londoners.

Lunch The cutting-edge contemporary **Serpentine Gallery** (▷ 84) holds an annual competition for its temporary summer café building. Alternatively, historic **Kensington Palace Orangery** (▷ 92) built in 1704 is open for lunch all year round.

Mid-afternoon Explore Kensington Palace to enjoy panelled rooms, stunning painted ceilings, a peak at Queen Victoria's childhood rooms and outfits worn by both the Queen and Princess Diana.

Dinner Seek out Old Court Place, off Kensington Church Street, and join plenty of Londoners to enjoy an old favourite, **Maggie Jones's** (▷ 92); reliable British dishes in a relaxed atmosphere at reasonable prices.

Evening Experience some London nightlife. It is a short taxi ride to sample the latest music at **Notting Hill Arts Club** (▷ 91), have a laugh at the **Comedy Store** (▷ 79), or listen to jazz at the **Jazz Café** (▷ 105).

Top 25

►►►

Banqueting House ▷ 64
The only surviving part of Henry VIII's great Whitehall Palace.

British Museum ▷ 48
Britain's largest museum unrivalled for the variety and quality of treasures.

Buckingham Palace ▷ 62
The Queen's London home is a symbol of British monarchy.

Natural History Museum ▷ 86 More than 67 million items, ranging from whales to insects and meteorites.

National Portrait Gallery ▷ 67 The most comprehensive portrait collection of remarkable people.

National Gallery ▷ 66
Home of the nation's permanent collection of Western European art.

Portobello Road Market ▷ 97 For anything and everything, fake or sublimely real.

◄◄◄

Royal Botanic Gardens, Kew ▷ 98 A royal palace, glasshouses, trees, gardens.

St. James's Park ▷ 68
The most attractive of all London's green spaces.

St. Pauls Cathedral ▷ 37
Sir Christopher Wren's masterpiece.

Science Museum ▷ 87
Celebrates and explains humankind's greatest scientific achievements.

Sir John Soane's Museum ▷ 50 Soane's fascinating collection in his houses.

Somerset House ▷ 51
Outstanding art collections and Georgian architecture.

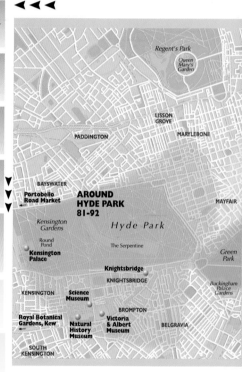

Tate Britain ▷ 69
The world's largest collection of British art from 1500 to the present day.

Tate Modern ▷ 26
A stimulating collection of international modern art from 1900 to the present.

Thames River Cruise ▷ 70 Get a whole new perspective on London from the water.

►►►

These pages are a quick guide to the Top 25, which are described in more detail later. Here they are listed alphabetically and the tinted background shows the area they are in.

►►►

Greenwich ▷ 96
Perfect for a family day out, with shops, a market and Britain's maritime past.

Houses of Parliament ▷ 65 Amazing headquarters of national government for more than 700 years.

Kensington Palace and Gardens ▷ 84 Private palace for royals set in peaceful gardens.

Museum of London ▷ 36
Trace the City's development from prehistoric times to the 21st century.

London Eye ▷ 24
London's most visible amusement soars above the River Thames.

Knightsbridge Shopping Spree ▷ 85 Harrods takes main stage among dazzling shop windows.

◄◄◄

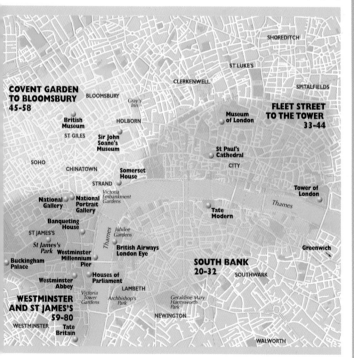

SHOREDITCH

ST LUKE'S

CLERKENWELL

SPITALFIELDS

COVENT GARDEN TO BLOOMSBURY 45–58

BLOOMSBURY

Gray's Inn

HOLBORN

British Museum

ST GILES

Sir John Soane's Museum

Museum of London

FLEET STREET TO THE TOWER 33–44

SOHO

CHINATOWN

Somerset House

STRAND

St Paul's Cathedral

CITY

National Gallery

National Portrait Gallery

Victoria Embankment Gardens

Tower of London

Banqueting House

Tate Modern

Thames

ST JAMES'S

St James's Park

Jubilee Gardens

Westminster Millennium Pier

British Airways London Eye

Greenwich

Buckingham Palace

Thames

SOUTH BANK 20–32

SOUTHWARK

Westminster Abbey

Houses of Parliament

LAMBETH

WESTMINSTER AND ST JAMES'S 59–80

Victoria Tower Gardens

Archbishop's Park

Geraldine Mary Harmsworth Park

WESTMINSTER

Tate Britain

NEWINGTON

WALWORTH

Tower of London ▷ 38
England's finest medieval fort encapsulates London's history.

Victoria and Albert Museum ▷ 88
One of the world's best collections of decorative arts.

Westminster Abbey ▷ 72
London's largest surviving medieval church; the setting for coronations.

►►►

Shopping

If England really is a nation of shopkeepers, then London is the head office. You can hunt down almost anything if you are determined enough. London has long been the world's marketplace and you'll find saris and spices as easily as rare reggae records, depending on the district—it really does pay to explore beyond the West End. For shoppers, the choice ranges from vibrant street markets to legendary world-famous department stores and from off-beat boutiques to smart galleries of paintings and antiques.

Hip and Traditional

It is the range that excites visitors, whether in antiques, classics or cutting-edge contemporary. London has outrageous fashion, bolstered by the annual crop of imaginative art, fashion and design school graduates. By contrast, long-established shopping streets, such as Oxford Street and Kensington High Street, offer mass-market goods, while markets such as Camden Lock and Portobello Road are eclectic, ethnic and inexpensive.

Buying a London Memory

London's souvenirs range from tatty to tasteful. Ever since the Swinging Sixties, anything with a Union Jack flag on it has sold well, from T-shirts

BEST OF BRITISH

Take home some British souvenirs with a difference. You can buy beautifully crafted umbrellas and walking sticks from James Smith & Sons (✉ 53 New Oxford Street, WC1). For a good British cheese buy a Stilton, all ready and packed, from Paxton & Whitfield (✉ 93 Jermyn Street, SW1). If you want to try some British recipes go to Books for Cooks (✉ 4 Blenheim Crescent, W11) for a large selection of cookbooks. Tea addicts should head to The Tea House (✉ 15A Neale Street, WC2) for a choice of blends and some stylish teapots. English herbs, oils and toiletries from Culpeper Herbalists (✉ 8 The Market, WC2) make great presents.

Shopping is diverse; from the fun of Chinatown and Portobello Market to the chaos of Oxford Street

to garish hats. For high quality, go to museums' in-house shops. Gifts at the shop in Buckingham Palace Mews include the Queen Victoria range of china, a mini throne for a charm bracelet or a guardsman puppet. The Victoria and Albert Museum, British Museum and National Gallery also stock quality items inspired by their diverse collections—you can do a full-scale family gift shop at any of these. The Design Museum offers immensely chic designer goods while the Museum of London is particularly good for souvenirs and books about London. At the National Portrait Gallery, you will find books on historical figures and British history, as well as a good supply of post-cards and posters.

The Ultimate British Buy

Go to St. James's or Knightsbridge to purchase traditional British-made goods such as tweed jackets, flat caps and handmade shoes or delicate fragrances, elegant china, floral printed fabrics and, of course, cashmere sweaters. London has long-established businesses with world-wide reputations. Visit Burlington Arcade for its specialist upscale shops in an historic set-ting. Burberry and Aquascutum are synony-mous with raincoats. Harrods has been trading for some 150 years; Selfridges was the coun-try's first department store; and Liberty fabrics are still exotic and luxurious. Their January and July sales are major events on any serious shoppers' calendar.

Hamleys toys are a must for kids, and adults won't resist the delicacies at Fauchon. A beadle, Burlington Arcade

SHOP THE SHOP

Charles Dickens would recognize many London shops. Burlington Arcade, off Piccadilly, is an 18th-century covered shopping mall, with a liveried beadle to maintain decorum. Many shops display the royal insignia, showing that they supply members of the royal household with everything from brushes to jewels (www.royalwarrant. org). For instance, John Lobb (✉ 88 Jermyn Street, SW1Y) custom-makes shoes and boots for the royal family—and for you, at a price.

Shopping by Theme

Whether you're looking for a department store, a quirky boutique, or something in between, you'll find it all in London. On this page shops are listed by theme. For a more detailed write-up, see the individual listings in London by Area.

ART AND ANTIQUES

Agnews (▷ 77)
Antiquarius (▷ 104)
Bonham's (▷ 54)
Christie's (▷ 77)
Contemporary Applied Arts (▷ 54)
The Fine Art Society (▷ 54)
Grays Antique Market (▷ 54)
Kensington Church Street (▷ 90)
Sotheby's (▷ 55)
Spink & Son (▷ 55)

BOOKS

Bernard Quaritch (▷ 54)
Books for Cooks (▷ 104)
Daunt Books (▷ 104)
Forbidden Planet (▷ 54)
Hatchards (▷ 77)
Maggs Brothers (▷ 77)
Stanfords (▷ 55)
Waterstone's (▷ 77)
Zwemmer Arts Bookshop (▷ 55)

DEPARTMENT STORES

Fortnum & Mason (▷ 77)
General Trading Company (▷ 90)
Harrods (▷ 90)
Harvey Nichols (▷ 90)
John Lewis (▷ 54)
Liberty (▷ 55)
Marks & Spencer (▷ 90)
Peter Jones (▷ 90)
Selfridges (▷ 55)

FASHION

Anderson & Sheppard (▷ 54)
Brora (▷ 104)
Brown's (▷ 54)
Designer Warehouse Sales (▷ 104)
Jigsaw (▷ 54)
Jimmy Choo (▷ 90)
Koh Samui (▷ 54)
Lulu Guinness (▷ 90)
Massimo Dutti (▷ 55)
Turnbull & Asser (▷ 77)
Urban Outfitters (▷ 90)

FOOD AND DRINK

Berry Bros & Rudd (▷ 77)
Carluccio's (▷ 54)
Haynes Hanson & Clark (▷ 90)
Neal's Yard Dairy (▷ 55)
Rococo (▷ 104)
Villandry (▷ 55)

HEALTH AND BEAUTY

Neal's Yard Remedies (▷ 55)
The Sanctuary (▷ 55)

HOMEWARE

Aram Designs Ltd (▷ 54)
Ceramica Blue (▷ 104)
Designer's Guild (▷ 104)
Heal's (▷ 54)
Jeanette Hayhurst (▷ 90)
Thomas Goode Ltd (▷ 77)
Waterford Wedgwood (▷ 77)

STREET MARKETS

Bermondsey Market (▷ 104)
Borough Market (▷ 27)
Camden Marktets (▷ 104)
Camden Passage (▷ 104)
Leadenhall Market (▷ 43)
Petticoat Lane (▷ 43)
Portobello Market (▷ 97)
Spitalfields Market (▷ 43)

London by Night

When darkness falls, London's pace doesn't let up; the capital's nightlife is world class. Eager visitors from around the world and London's style-conscious citizens add to the lively mix in London's nightclubs and bars. Licensing laws were revised in 2006, permitting many venues, from pubs to clubs, to stay open longer. But the smoking ban of 2007 saw smokers relegated to the pavement.

Entertainment
The choice is astounding: London has about 150 theatres, while 400 concerts take place each week in all kinds of buildings. Then there are opera, ballet and theatre seasons, and festivals often set in buildings otherwise closed to public.

Summer Living
Come summer, London's outdoors comes into its own. Londoners enjoy concerts in settings such as Hampton Court Palace, Kenwood House, Hyde Park and Kew Gardens. The music ranges from classical and opera to jazz and rock-and-roll. Bars, pubs and cafés spill onto the streets, and many serve good food.

Clubs and Bars
Year-round the diversity of the club scene is legendary and with many changing themes, check before you go. There are tried-and-tested venues for older clubbers and a host of pulsing new wave options. London's extensive bar scene ranges from the smart Savoy to all-night hip AKA.

Whatever you fancy, it's all here; thrilling funfairs, traditional pubs, trendy clubs or more sedate theatres

---

WALK THE WALK

The 2km (1-mile) long stretch of riverside on the South Bank between Westminster and London bridges bustles by night, as well as by day. The London Eye (▷ 24) is magical after dark. On the opposite bank, illuminated landmarks include the Houses of Parliament and Somerset House. At Oxo Tower Wharf, go to the top floor for a drink or a meal. There are few better views of London. Admire Tate Modern (open until 10pm Friday and Saturday) and the Globe. Rest your feet at a riverside pub.

Eating Out

London's reputation for food ranks with the best in the world—more than 40 restaurants boast one or more Michelin stars. The public has become discerning, chefs have high profiles and London creates its own culinary trends. Top restaurants celebrate traditional British food by using quality British ingredients to create lighter versions of familiar specials.

Cafés, Brasseries and Bistros
Multicultural London offers exciting restaurants serving more than 50 different cuisines from cutting-edge contemporary to Middle Eastern food. The more substantial cafés often stay open all day. Many are either in historic buildings or notable contemporary ones.

Fast Food and Restaurant Chains
Forget McDonald's: for better burgers try the Gourmet Burger Kitchens. Yo!Sushi, Wagamama and Masala Zone provide Asian food, while Pizza Express is a good pizza chain.

Pubs and Bars
You'll find Irish bars, sports bars, traditional street corner pubs and slick futuristic bars. Some are in warrens of Tudor rooms; others take pride in their grand Victorian and Edwardian decorations. Those that have reinvented themselves as gastropubs combine a fine setting with quality drinks and food.

Afternoon Tea
The great British institution is still widely available in hotels and tearooms from about 2 or 3pm. There are many variations, but it always includes a pot of tea and something to eat, which can vary from sandwiches and cakes to cream teas.

Dress Code
In the past the British loved to dress for dinner but these days only the most formal restaurants demand a jacket and tie, but customers should dress appropriately to eat in upscale restaurants.

Inside or out, casual or opulent, London's cafés and restaurants will provide the solution to all occasions

Restaurants by Cuisine

There are restaurants to suit all tastes and budgets in London. On this page they are listed by cuisine. For a more detailed description of each restaurant, see London by Area.

ASIAN

Amaya (▷ 92)
Benares (▷ 57)
Eat-Thai.net (▷ 57)
Imli (▷ 57)
K–10 (▷ 44)
Masala Zone (▷ 58)
Nobu (▷ 92)
Rasa Samudra (▷ 58)
Royal China (▷ 92)
Salloos (▷ 92)
Shochu (▷ 58)
Tamarind (▷ 80)
Wagamama (▷ 58)

BRASSERIES/BRUNCH

Babylon (▷ 106)
Christopher's (▷ 57)
Flaneur Food Hall (▷ 44)
Joe Allen (▷ 57)
Vincent Rooms (▷ 80)

BRITISH AND MODERN

Le Café Anglais (▷ 106)
Cicada (▷ 44)
The Glasshouse (▷ 106)
Maggie Jones's (▷ 92)
Medcalf (▷ 106)
Ottolenghi (▷ 106)
Oxo Tower Restaurant (▷ 32)
The Portrait Restaurant (▷ 80)
Rules (▷ 58)
St. John (▷ 44)
The Wolseley (▷ 80)

EUROPEAN

The Admiralty (▷ 57)
Baltic (▷ 32)
Bevis Monks Restaurant (▷ 44)
Blue Print Café (▷ 32)
Cantina Vinopolis (▷ 32)
Club Gascon (▷ 44)
Gaby's (▷ 57)
Haz (▷ 44)
Hibiscus (▷ 57)
Magdalen (▷ 32)
Providores & Tapa Room (▷ 106)
Tom Aikens (▷ 92)
Villandry (▷ 106)
Wild Honey (▷ 58)
Zizzi (▷ 58)

FAMOUS CHEFS

Fifteen (▷ 106)
Le Gavroche (▷ 92)
Greenhouse (▷ 80)
Maze (▷ 92)
Rhodes Twenty Four (▷ 44)
The Square (▷ 58)

FISH AND VEGETARIAN

Big Chill Bar (▷ 106)
Livebait (▷ 32)
The Place Below (▷ 44)
World Food Café (▷ 58)

GASTROPUBS/BARS

The Anchor (▷ 32)
Anchor & Hope (▷ 32)
Detroit (▷ 57)
The Eagle (▷ 44)
Gun (▷ 106)
Lowlander (▷ 57)
Peasant (▷ 44)

INTERNATIONAL

Gaucho (▷ 80)

LIGHTER BITES

Inn the Park (▷ 80)
Kensington Palace Orangery (▷ 92)
Paul (▷ 58)
Tate Modern Café (▷ 32)

If You Like...

However you'd like to spend your time in London, these top suggestions should help you tailor your ideal visit. Each sight or listing has a fuller write-up in London by Area.

SERIOUS RETAIL THERAPY

Start on the ground floor of Harrods (▷ 90) and work up, collecting Harrods shopping bags.
Be girlie: spend a whole day in Harvey Nichols (▷ 90) or Selfridges (▷ 55).
Search Antiquarius (▷ 104) for indulgent period accessories.
Submerge yourself on a weekend into the five markets of the Camden Markets (▷ 104).
Tempt your tastebuds at Borough Market's (▷ 27) organic and artisan food stalls.

EXOTIC INDIAN FOOD

Find Kerala dishes at Rasa Samudra (▷ 58).
Chew a meat meal at the northwest frontier Salloos (▷ 92).
Sink into sumptuous rich Mughal food at Tamarind (▷ 80).
Luxuriate in Uttar Pradesh delicacies at Benares (▷ 57).
Enjoy the real taste of authentic Indian food at the top of the range Amaya (▷ 92).

A MEAL WITH A VIEW

Book at the Portrait Restaurant atop the National Portrait Gallery (▷ 67).
Rendezvous at the Blueprint Café (▷ 32), upstairs at the Design Museum.
Go to Canary Wharf to eat at the waterside Gun (▷ 106).
Splash out at Rhodes Twenty Four (▷ 44), with a cocktail 18 floors above at Vertigo 42.
Eat informally amid trees and flamingos at rooftop Babylon (▷ 106).

Camden Market for bargains, followed by Harrods food hall or an elegant restaurant to tempt the tastebuds

Go ahead and spoil your-self at one of London's luxury hotels

AN INDULGENT HOTEL ROOM

Enjoy perfect decoration in Hazlitt's (▷ 112) 18th-century houses.

Imbibe grand hotel chic at the small, perfectly maintained Ritz (▷ 112).

Pack to parade through the lobby to your room at the Dorchester (▷ 112).

Find chic contemporary aesthetics at the Halkin (▷ 112).

Pamper yourself with a Thames view room at the Savoy (▷ 112) and enjoy huge bathroom showerheads.

A BREATH OF FRESH AIR

Roam Hampstead Heath (▷ 100) and visit Kenwood House (▷ 100).

Climb high in Greenwich Park (▷ 96) to enjoy London views.

Enjoy seasonal splendour at the Royal Botanic Gardens, Kew (▷ 98).

Go boating in Regent's Park (▷ 101) and visit the zoo.

Do the great central London royal park walk: through St. James's (▷ 68), Green (▷ 75) and Hyde parks (▷ 89), then Kensington Gardens (▷ 84).

For a great night combine excellent jazz with amazing cocktails (above). British Museum (below)

NIGHT-TIME FUN ABOUT TOWN

Jazz Café, Jazz After Dark and Pizza Express Jazz Club (▷ 56) serve up quality jazz.

Check out Canvas (▷ 105) and the cluster of funky clubs at King's Cross.

Drink and dance the night away at The End (▷ 56).

Barfly (▷ 105) in Camden showcases the indie scene with several acts nightly.

Head across the river to the Ministry of Sound (▷ 31) for dependable clubbing.

WATCHING THE BANK BALANCE

The Tate Modern (below) opened in 2000

Stay at funky Ashlee House (▷ 109) youth hostel.
Eat at Gaby's (▷ 57) on Charing Cross Road.
Go to a free concert in a church such as St. Margaret, Lothbury (▷ 41).
Buy your theatre tickets at 'tkts' in Leicester Square (▷ 79).
Visit a free museum such as the British Museum (▷ 48).

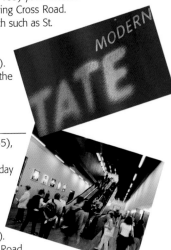

SHOPPING FOR ANTIQUES

View a sale at Sotheby's (▷ 55), then bid on your preferred lot.
Spend a Wednesday or Saturday at Camden Passage (▷ 104).
Get up early on Friday for Bermondsey Market (▷ 104).
Cruise the specialty shops in Kensington Church Street (▷ 90).
Spend Saturday at Portobello Road (▷ 97).

PEAKING INSIDE LONDONER'S HOMES

Dr. Johnson's house (▷ 40), where he compiled his dictionary.
Sir John Soane's two houses (▷ 50), filled with his antiquities.
Handel House (▷ 52), the German composer's home for 26 years.
Buckingham Palace (▷ 62), the Queen's London home.
Spencer House (▷ 75), the aristocratic Spencer family's mansion.

Sir John Soane's Museum (above). Bric-a-brac stalls at Portobello Road Market (below)

KEEPING THE KIDS HAPPY

Handle objects at the hands-on tables in the British Museum (▷ 48).
Climb the steps to the top of St. Paul's (▷ 37).
Go boating in Regent's Park (▷ 101).
Have a 'science night' sleepover at the Science Museum (▷ 87).

Sights	24–28	**SOUTH BANK**
Walk	29	
Entertainment and Nightlife	31	
Restaurants	32	

Sights	36–41	**FLEET STREET TO THE TOWER**
Walk	42	
Shopping	43	
Entertainment and Nightlife	43	
Restaurants	44	

Sights	48–53	**COVENT GARDEN TO BLOOMSBURY**
Shopping	54–55	
Entertainment and Nightlife	56	
Restaurants	57–58	

Sights	62–75	**WESTMINSTER AND ST. JAMES'S**
Walk	76	
Shopping	77	
Entertainment and Nightlife	79	
Restaurants	80	

Sights	84–89	**AROUND HYDE PARK**
Shopping	90	
Entertainment and Nightlife	91	
Restaurants	92	

Sights	96–102	**FARTHER AFIELD**
Walk	103	
Shopping	104	
Entertainment and Nightlife	105	
Restaurants	106	

Start exploring London by crossing the river to its historic entertainment hub where the Tudors had their theatres. Entertainment ranks highly here—from the Design Museum to the London Aquarium, via Southwark Cathedral and the Royal National Theatre.

Sights	24–28
Walk	29
Entertainment and Nightlife	31
Restaurants	32

Top 25

London Eye ▷ 24
Tate Modern ▷ 26

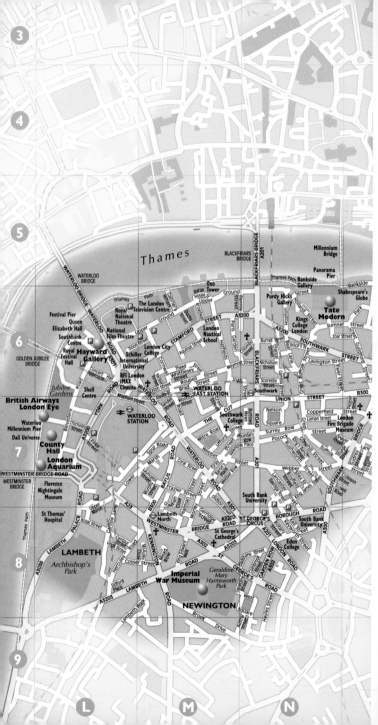

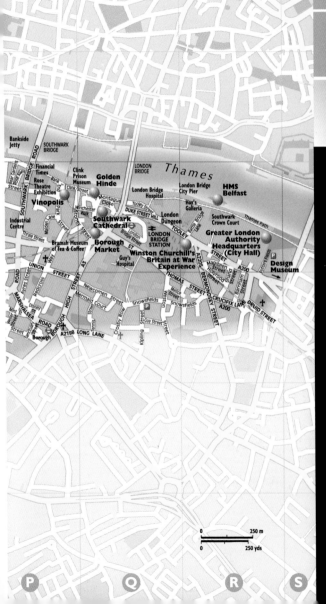

Bankside Jetty

SOUTHWARK BRIDGE

SOUTHWARK BRIDGE ROAD

Bear Gardens

Rose Alley

New Globe Walk

Emerson Street

Park Street

Financial Times

Rose Theatre Exhibition

Vinopolis

Clink Prison Museum

Clink Street

Bank End

Golden Hinde

LONDON BRIDGE

Thames

Montague Close

Winchester Walk

Stoney Street

Cathedral Street

Maiden Lane

Redcross Way

Thrale Street

Industrial Centre

Branah Museum of Tea & Coffee

Southwark Cathedral

Borough Market

UNION STREET

A3

BOROUGH HIGH STREET

Disney Place

Newcomen Street

Mermaid Court

Crosby Row

LONG LANE

A219B

MARSHALSEA ROAD

Mint Street

Southwark Bridge Road

Lant Street

Weller Street

Borough

Ayres Street

London Bridge Hospital

DUKE STREET HILL

London Dungeon

TOOLEY STREET

LONDON BRIDGE STATION

St Thomas Street

Guy's Hospital

Winston Churchill's Britain at War Experience

Snowsfields

Kipling Street

Guy Street

London Bridge City Pier

Hay's Galleria

HMS Belfast

Thames Path

Southwark Crown Court

Battle Bridge Lane

Tooley Street

A200

Greater London Authority Headquarters (City Hall)

Potters Fields

Morgan's Lane

Gainsford Street

Shad Thames

Design Museum

A200

Queen Elizabeth Street

THOMAS STREET

A2206

BERMONDSEY STREET

Melior Street

Snowsfields

Magdalen Street

Holyrood Street

Weston Street

CRUCIFIX LANE

DRUID STREET

Bermondsey Street

---

0   250 m

0   250 yds

P   Q   R   S

London Eye

HIGHLIGHTS

● Panoramic views across
the city in every direction
● On a clear day you can
see for 40km (25 miles)
● Spotting Thames landmarks
● Aerial view of Palace of
Westminster

TIPS

● It is best to book ahead,
although not essential.
● Night riders enjoy the
London lights.
● Book ahead to gain free
admission for children under
five.

**London's most visible attraction, soaring
135m (443ft) above the South Bank of
the Thames, is the world's largest observation wheel and affords spectacular
views of the city.**

Riding high Passengers ride in one of the 32 capsules that rotate smoothly through 360 degrees in
a slow-moving, 30-minute flight. Each capsule is
fully enclosed and comfortably holds 25 people.
Because the capsules are secured on the outside
of the wheel (rather than hung from it like a Ferris
Wheel), views through the large glass windows are
totally unobstructed. Passengers can walk freely
inside the capsules, which are kept level by a
motorized motion stability system—although seat-
ing is provided. Each capsule is in touch with the
ground via camera and radio links. The wheel is in

The London Eye (right) and the wonderful view along the River Thames from within one of the 32 observation capsules (left)

constant motion, revolving continuously at 0.26m (0.85ft) per second, a quarter of the average walking speed, enabling passengers to walk straight on and off the moving capsules. After dark, the trees lining the approach to the London Eye are bathed in green lights, while the boarding platform appears to float on a cloud of blue light.

Revolutionary design Conceived by David Marks and Julia Barfield to celebrate the millennium, the Eye represents the turning of the century and is a universal and ancient symbol of regeneration. It took seven years and the expertize of people from five European countries for their design to be realized. The Eye marks the start of the riverside Jubilee Walk that reaches right up to Tower Bridge. It has also helped to revitalize a forgotten corner of London.

THE BASICS

www.londoneye.com

⊞ L7

✉ Riverside Gardens, next to County Hall, SE1

☎ 0870 990 8883; booking 0870 500 0600

🕐 Jun–end Sep daily 10–9; Oct–end May daily 10–8

🍴 Riverfront cafés

🚇 Waterloo, Westminster, Embankment, Charing Cross

🚆 Waterloo

♿ Very good. Boarding ramp available for wheelchair users

💷 Expensive

Tate Modern

The exterior (left) and interior (right) of Tate Modern. An exhibit with a difference (middle)

THE BASICS

www.tate.org.uk

⊞ N6

✉ Bankside, SE1

☎ 020 7887 8888

🕐 Sun–Thu 10–6, Fri–Sat 10–10

🍴 Cafés, restaurant

Ⓕ Blackfriars, Southwark

Ⓕ Blackfriars, London Bridge

♿ Very good

💷 Free, charge for some special exhibitions

❓ Full educational schedule. Choice of free daily audio tours

HIGHLIGHTS

Although diplays change, look out for works by:

● Pablo Picasso
● Claude Monet
● Henri Matisse
● Constantin Brancusi
● Jackson Pollock
● Mark Rothko
● Bridget Riley
● Marcel Duchamp
● Andy Warhol

The national collection of modern art fills the magnificent spaces of George Gilbert Scott's monumental Bankside Power Station by the Thames, making it a radical focus for the long strip of riverside arts emporia.

World-class art On a par with the Metropolitan Museum of Modern Art in New York, the collection that once shared space with the British collection (▷ 69) now blossoms in its own huge spaces. Swiss architects Herzog & de Meuron have created an exciting contemporary structure within the handsome brick building, making it ideal for exhibiting large-scale works of art in an innovative way. Gallery events, cafés, a big shop and a rooftop restaurant complete the total package for a great day on the South Bank or, using the Millennium Bridge designed by Caro and Rogers, a combination with city sightseeing.

20th century and more The most influential artists of the 20th century are all represented, including Picasso, Matisse, Dali, Duchamp, Rodin, Gabo and Warhol—as well as British artists such as Bacon, Hodgkin, Hockney and Caro. Together they represent all the major periods and movements of the 20th century, from Surrealism to Conceptual Art. Four suites of rooms, each devoted to one subject, mix together pieces from various periods. A total rehang of these permanent galleries in 2006 brought mellow Rothkos into focus and cast Monet as an abstract forerunner.

More to See

BOROUGH MARKET
Browse 18th-century Borough Market's food stalls for hand-crafted bread, cheeses and organic produce.
➕ Q6 ✉ Southwark Street, SE1 ⏰ Thu–Sat 🚇 London Bridge 🚆 London Bridge

CITY HALL
Norman Foster designed the Mayor of London's headquarters.
➕ R6 ✉ The Queen's Wharf, SE1 🚆 London Bridge

COUNTY HALL
A 1920s listed building houses the Dali Universe and London Aquarium (▷ 28).
➕ L7 ✉ County Hall, Riverside Building, Westminster Bridge Road, SE1 🍴 Cafés, restaurants 🚆 Westminster

DESIGN MUSEUM
www.designmuseum.org
Founded by design guru Sir Terence Conran. Good temporary exhibitions.
➕ S7 ✉ 28 Shad Thames, SE1 ☎ 0870 909 9009 ⏰ Daily 10–5.45, Fri until 9 🍴 Café, restaurant 🚆 Tower Hill, London Bridge 🚆 London Bridge 👣 Moderate

GOLDEN HINDE
www.goldenhinde.org
The exact replica of Sir Francis Drake's galleon in which he circumnavigated the globe between 1577 and 1580. Take a guided tour.
➕ Q6 ✉ St. Mary Overie Dock, Cathedral Street, SE1 ☎ 0870 011 8700 ⏰ Usually daily 10 until dusk, but hours vary 🚆 London Bridge 🚆 London Bridge 👣 Moderate

HAYWARD GALLERY
www.hayward.org.uk
Revitalized building matched by its exhibition programming.
➕ L6 ✉ Belvedere Road, SE1 ☎ 08703 800 400 ⏰ Daily 10–6 during exhibitions, Fri until 9 🚆 Waterloo 🚆 Waterloo 👣 Moderate

HMS BELFAST
www.iwm.org.uk
Clamber up, down and around this 1938 war cruiser, visiting the cabins, gun turrets, bridge and boiler-room.
➕ R6 ✉ Morgan's Lane, Tooley Street, SE1 ☎ 020 7940 6300 ⏰ Mar–end Oct daily

The glass structure of City Hall, office to the Mayor of London

The Golden Hinde

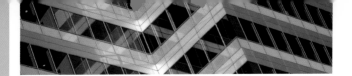

10–6; Nov–end Feb 10–5 🍴 Café
🚇 London Bridge 🚉 London Bridge
🎫 Moderate; children under 16 free

IMPERIAL WAR MUSEUM

www.iwm.org.uk
The museum focuses on the social
impact of 20th-century warfare
through film, painting and sound
archives. The Holocaust Museum is
not suitable for children.
➕ M8 ✉ Lambeth Road, SE1 ☎ 020
7416 5320 🕐 Daily 10–6 🍴 Restaurant,
café 🚇 Lambeth North, Elephant & Castle,
Waterloo 🚉 Waterloo 🎫 Free

LONDON AQUARIUM

www.londonaquarium.co.uk
More than 3,000 forms of marine life
fill this aquatic spectacular.
➕ L7 ✉ County Hall, SE1 ☎ 020 7967
8000 🕐 Daily 10–6, school hols until 7
🚇 Westminster 🎫 Expensive

SOUTHWARK CATHEDRAL

www.southwarkanglican.org/cathedral
A fine stone building powerfully
atmospheric of its medieval origins,
despite much rebuilding; fine choir
and monuments.
➕ Q6 ✉ London Bridge, SE1 ☎ 020
7367 6700 🕐 Daily 8–6 🚇 London Bridge
🚉 London Bridge 🎫 Moderate

VINOPOLIS

www.vinopolis.co.uk
A warren of rooms devoted to the
world's wine-growing regions. Films,
experts, tastings and a restaurant.
➕ P6 ✉ 1 Bank End, SE1 ☎ 0870 241
4040 🕐 Mon–Fri 12–10, Sat 11–9, Sun
12–6. Prebooking essential 🚇 London
Bridge 🚉 London Bridge 🎫 Expensive,
includes audio guide and tastings

WINSTON CHURCHILL'S BRITAIN AT WAR EXPERIENCE

www.britainatwar.co.uk
A tribute to ordinary people who lived
their lives against the backdrop of air
raids, the blackout, rationing and evac-
uation in World War II.
➕ R6 ✉ 64–66 Tooley Street, SE1 ☎ 020
7403 3171 🕐 Apr–end Sep daily 10–6;
Oct–end Mar 10–5 🚇 London Bridge
🚉 London Bridge 🎫 Moderate

HMS Belfast with Tower Bridge in the background

The South Bank

This walk hugs the riverbank and enjoys superb views across London's core, while taking in many of the city's most famous attractions.

DISTANCE: 2.5km (1.5 miles) approx. **ALLOW:** 2–3 hours depending on visits

START

TOWER BRIDGE 🚩 S6
🚇 Tower Hill 🚆 London Bridge

END

ROYAL FESTIVAL HALL (▷ 31)
🚇 Charing Cross 🚆 Westminster

SOUTH BANK

WALK

❶ Begin the walk at Tower Bridge, linking the Tower of London and the Thames Path, from where there are stupendous high-level views across London.

❽ Cross the Thames by Hungerford footbridge for Charing Cross, or Westminster Bridge if you want to see the Houses of Parliament (▷ 65) at Westminster.

❼ After Southwark bridge find Shakespeare's Globe Theatre (▷ 31) and Tate Modern (▷ 26). The riverfront widens at the South Bank arts complex (▷ 31); the London Eye (▷ 24), Saatchi Gallery and London Aquarium (▷ 28) lie beyond.

❷ Stroll eastward among the old warehouses and new restaurants of Shad Thames to find Anthony Donaldson's Waterfall sculpture in Tower Bridge Piazza on the right.

❸ Along the riverside, look out for Eduardo Paolozzi's sculpture and you can visit the Design Museum (▷ 27), which is at Shad Thames; quality shop and café.

❻ Past London Bridge take in Southwark Cathedral (▷ 28, worth going inside) and, after the *Golden Hinde* (▷ 27) replica galleon, a wall and rose window of the 14th-century Winchester Palace's Great Hall.

❹ West of Tower Bridge, just past the shimmering City Hall (▷ 27), the riverbank path leads to HMS *Belfast* (▷ 27) and Hay's Galleria where you will find more cafés.

❺ Outside the Cottons Centre is a pavilion where a map plots the buildings along City view.

29

Entertainment and Nightlife

IMAX CINEMA
www.bfi.org.uk/imax
A 480-seat cinema in a space-age balloon showing exhilarating 2-D and 3-D movies.
🚇 L6 ✉ South Bank, SE1
☎ 0870 787 2525
Ⓜ Embankment, Waterloo

MINISTRY OF SOUND
www.ministryofsound.com
Glamorous and justly popular club housed in a prison-like building.
🚇 N8 ✉ 103 Gaunt Street, SE1 ☎ 020 7378 6528
Ⓜ Elephant and Castle

NATIONAL FILM THEATRE (NFT)
www.bfi.org.uk/nft
Diverse agenda on three screens. Focus of the annual London Film Festival.
🚇 L6 ✉ South Bank, SE1
☎ 020 7928 3232
Ⓜ Embankment, Waterloo

OLD VIC
www.oldvictheatre.com
This sumptuous Victorian theatre stages productions that are often acclaimed.
🚇 M7 ✉ The Cut, Waterloo Road, SE1 ☎ 0870 060 6628
Ⓜ Waterloo, Southwark

PURCELL ROOM
www.rfh.org.uk
An intimate space for chamber music, accompanied singers, solo singers, musicians and more.
🚇 L6 ✉ South Bank, SE1 8XR ☎ 0871 663 2500
Ⓜ Embankment, Waterloo

QUEEN ELIZABETH HALL
www.rfh.org.uk
Come here for small orchestras, bands, small-scale opera, piano recitals and dance.
🚇 L6 ✉ South Bank, SE1
☎ 0871 663 2500
Ⓜ Embankment, Waterloo

ROYAL FESTIVAL HALL
www.rfh.org.uk
Largescale orchestral concerts, plus jazz and ballet. The grand reopening in June 2007 after refurbishment included Larry Kirkegaard's accoustics.
🚇 L6 ✉ South Bank, SE1
☎ 0871 663 2500
Ⓜ Embankment, Waterloo

ROYAL NATIONAL THEATRE (RNT)
www.nationaltheatre.org.uk
Home of the National Theatre company, it has

THEATRE TIPS
If you care about where you sit, go in person and peruse the plan. For an evening 'Sold out' performance, it is worth waiting in line for returns; otherwise, try for a matinée. The most inexpensive seats may be far from the stage or uncomfortable, so take binoculars and a cushion. Londoners rarely dress up for the theatre anymore but they do order their intermission drinks before the play starts, and remain seated while they applaud.

three performance spaces; the Olivier, Lyttelton and Cottesloe all stage several productions in repertory.
🚇 L6 ✉ South Bank, SE1
☎ 020 7452 3000 Information and tours Ⓜ Embankment, Waterloo 🚊 Waterloo

SHAKESPEARE'S GLOBE
www.shakespeares-globe.org
A faithful reconstruction of the open-air Elizabethan playhouse where many of Shakespeare's plays were first performed. Performance season May to September; take a coat and rainhat.
🚇 P6 ✉ 21 New Globe Walk, SE1 ☎ 020 7401 9919
Ⓜ London Bridge, Mansion House

SOUTHBANK CENTRE
www.rfh.org.uk
Arts complex comprising the Royal Festival Hall, Queen Elizabeth Hall and Purcell Room. Currently under architect Rick Mather's refurbishment. See individual entries on this page.
🚇 L6 ✉ South Bank, SE1
☎ 0871 663 2500
Ⓜ Embankment, Waterloo

YOUNG VIC
www.youngvic.org
The new theatre providing a stage for one of London's most exciting troupes opened in 2006.
🚇 M7 ✉ The Cut, SE1
☎ 020 7922 2922
Ⓜ Waterloo, Southwark

Restaurants

RESTAURANTS

SOUTH BANK

PRICES

Prices are approximate, based on a 3-course meal for one person.

£££	over £60
££	£30–£60
£	under £30

THE ANCHOR (£)

Historic pub with excellent river views, black beams, faded plasterwork, a maze of tiny rooms and garden patio. Varied menu.

🚇 P6 ✉ Bankside, 34 Park Street, SE1 ☎ 020 7407 1577 🍴 Restaurant: Mon–Sat 12–3, 5–10 🚉 London Bridge

ANCHOR & HOPE (£)

Quality gastropub in great building. No reservations, so go early to enjoy very good British food before your theatre.

🚇 M7 ✉ 36 The Cut, SE1 ☎ 020 7928 9898 🍴 Tue–Sat 12–2.30, 6–10.30, Mon 6–10.30, Sun 12–3 🚉 Southwark, Waterloo

BALTIC (£)

www.balticrestaurant.co.uk Serious bar for cocktails; dramatic contemporary restaurant for modern Polish food. Jazz every Sun 7pm.

🚇 N6 ✉ 74 Blackfriars Road, SE1 ☎ 020 7928 1111 🍴 Mon–Sat 12–3, 6–11, Sun 12–10.30 🚉 Southwark

BLUEPRINT CAFÉ (££)

www.danddlondon.com Jeremy Lee's European dishes, stunning London views and an on-site museum.

🚇 S7 ✉ Design Museum, 28 Shad Thames, SE1 ☎ 020 7378 7031 🍴 Lunch 12–3, dinner 6–11 🚉 London Bridge

CANTINA VINOPOLIS (££)

www.acantinavinopolis.com Vivacious, wine-theme restaurant and bar. Mediterranean influenced dishes prepared in the open kitchen.

🚇 P6 ✉ 1 Bank End, SE1 ☎ 020 7940 8333 🍴 Mon–Sat 12–3, 6–10.30 🚉 London Bridge

---

RIVERSIDE EATING

London is exploiting the potential of its riverside views. Today, there is more than just the Admiralty (▷ 57) and the East End smugglers' pubs. The most spectacular views are from the Oxo Tower Restaurant (▷ this page) and the Tate Modern's roof-top restaurant at Bankside (▷ this page). There are lower but impressive views from the second-floor Blue Print Café (▷ this page) beside the Design Museum, Butler's Wharf, overlooking Tower Bridge and the City. For a more modest river view, try the Barley Mow pub (✉ 44 Narrow Street, E14), which overlooks the wider, curving Thames of the East End.

LIVEBAIT (£)

www.santeonline.co.uk/livebait This is the original near the Young and Old Vic theatres in The Cut. Good value set menu.

🚇 M7 ✉ 43 The Cut, SE1 ☎ 020 7928 7211 🍴 Mon–Sat 12–11, Sun 12.30–9 🚉 Southwark

MAGDALEN (£–££)

www.magdalenrestaurant.co.uk Tasty, seasonal dishes, often combining British heartiness and French sophistication.

🚇 R6 ✉ 152 Tooley Street, SE1 ☎ 020 7403 1342 🍴 Mon–Fri 12–2.30, 6.30–10.30 🚉 London Bridge

OXO TOWER BAR & RESTAURANT (££)

www.harveynichols.com Look out over London while eating, drinking or snacking on good European food. Plenty of outdoor tables; reservations essential.

🚇 M6 ✉ 8th Floor, Oxo Tower Wharf, Barge House Street, SE1 ☎ 020 7803 3888 🍴 Mon–Sat 12–3, Sun 12–3.30 🚉 Blackfriars

TATE MODERN CAFÉ (£)

www.tate.org.uk Take a break from the art to enjoy upscale café food and Thames views. (For a grand meal book at the roof-top restaurant.)

🚇 N6 ✉ Tate Modern, SE1 ☎ 020 7401 5014 🍴 Daily 10–6, until 9.30 Fri 🚉 Blackfriars, Southwark

London began in this area when the Romans established a port-city. For 2,000 years this has been 'the City' whose citizens have adapted to change. Their monuments—the Roman fort wall, churches— are joined by sparkling office towers.

Sights	36–41
Walk	42
Shopping	43
Entertainment and Nightlife	43
Restaurants	44

Top 25 **TOP 25**

Museum of London ▷ 36
St. Paul's Cathedral ▷ 37
The Tower of London ▷ 38

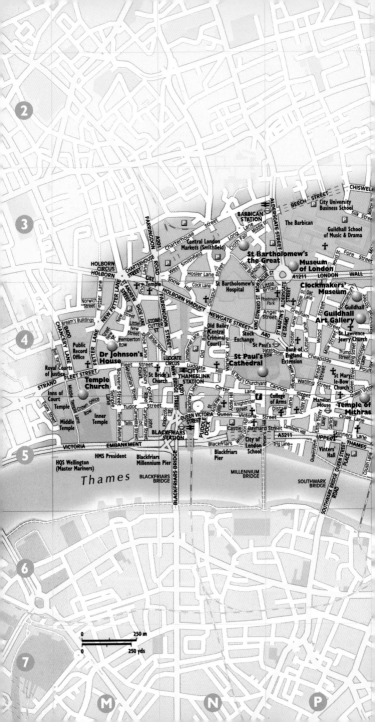

Q R S

Museum of London

TOP 25

Courtyard to the front of the Museum (left). Lord Mayor of London's State Coach (right)

THE BASICS

www.museumoflondon.org.uk

⊞ P3

✉ 150 London Wall, EC2

☎ 0870 444 3850

🕐 Mon–Sat 10–5.50, Sun 12–5.50. Closed 24–26 Dec, 1 Jan

🍴 Café

Ⓜ Barbican, Moorgate, St. Paul's

🚉 Moorgate

🚻 Excellent

💷 Free

❓ Full education schedule; audio tour

HIGHLIGHTS

● London Before London Gallery
● Hoard of 43 gold Roman coins
● Spitalfields Woman (Roman)
● Viking grave
● Fragments from the Eleanor Cross
● Model of Tudor London
● World City Gallery

A visit here is easily the best way to cruise through London's 2,000 years of history, pausing to see a Roman shoe, the Lord Mayor's State Coach or an old shop counter; and it is even built on the West Gate of London's Roman fort.

A museum for London This is the world's largest and most comprehensive city museum, opened in 1976 in a building by Powell and Moya. The collection combines the old Guildhall Museum's City antiquities with the London Museum's costumes and other culturally related objects. Lots of building work and redevelopment in the City since the l980s, allied with increased awareness about conservation, has ensured a steady flow of archaeological finds into the collection.

A museum about London The building is, appropriately, in the barbican of the Roman fort, and the rooms are laid out chronologically to keep the story clear. The London Before London gallery follows the story of prehistoric Londoners before Roman settlement. One of the most impressive galleries is Roman London, which explains the founding of Londinium in about AD50 until AD410 when the Roman army quit Britain. The World City galleries cover the period from the French Revolution to the outbreak of World War I. People make a city, so in every room it is Londoners who are really telling the story, whether it is through their Roman storage jars, their Tudor leather clothes or their Suffragette posters. An impressive £33 million redevelopment is now complete.

St. Paul's Cathedral is just as impressive and rewarding inside and out

St. Paul's Cathedral

To sneak into St. Paul's for afternoon evensong, and sit gazing up at the mosaics as the choir's voices soar, is to enjoy a moment of absolute peace and beauty. Go early or late to avoid the crowds.

Wren's London After the restoration of the monarchy in 1660, artistic patronage bloomed under Charles II. Then when the Great Fire of London destroyed four-fifths of the City in 1666, Christopher Wren took main stage, being appointed King's Surveyor-General in 1669. The spires and steeples of his 51 new churches (23 still stand) surrounded his masterpiece, St. Paul's.

The fifth St. Paul's This cathedral church for the diocese of London was founded in AD604 by King Ethelbert of Kent. The first four churches burned down. Wren's, built in stone and paid for with a special coal tax, was the first English cathedral built by a single architect, the only one with a dome, and the only one in the English baroque style. In 2005 it emerged from a total clean, pristine as the day the building was completed. Statues and memorials of Britain's famous crowd the interior and crypt—heros Wellington and Nelson, artists Turner and Reynolds, and Wren himself.

The climb The 530 steps to the top are worth the effort. Shallow steps rise to the Whispering Gallery for views of Sir James Thornhill's dome's frescoes and 19th-century mosaics. The external Stone Gallery has telescopes; above is the Golden Gallery.

THE BASICS

www.stpauls.co.uk

⊞ N4

✉ Ludgate Hill, EC4

☎ 020 7236 4128

◷ Mon–Sat 8.30–4. Galleries 9.30–3.30. Services include Mon–Sat 5, Sun 10.15, 3.15

🍴 Café in the crypt

Ⓠ St. Paul's

🚉 City Thameslink

♿ Very good

✋ Moderate

❓ Audio and guided tours (including Triforium tour); organ recitals

HIGHLIGHTS

● Sung evensong
● Frescoes and mosaics
● Wren's Great Model in the Triforium (upstairs)
● Triple-layered dome weighing 76,000 tons
● Jean Tijou's sanctuary gates
● Wellington's memorial
● *Light of the World*, Holman Hunt
● The view across London
● Wren's epitaph under the dome

FLEET STREET TO THE TOWER

TOP 25

37

The Tower of London

HIGHLIGHTS

- Medieval Palace
- Raleigh's room
- Imperial State Crown
- Tower ravens
- Grand Punch Bowl, 1829
- St. John's Chapel

TIPS

- Buy tickets in advance by calling 0870 950 4488 or online at www.hrp.org.uk.
- It's vital to arrive before opening time to avoid lines.
- Arrive well-fed, there's no café.

The restored rooms of Edward I's 13th-century palace bring the Tower alive as the royal palace and place of pageantry it was; for some, they are more interesting than the Crown Jewels.

Medieval glory The Tower of London is Britain's best medieval fortress. William the Conqueror (1066–87) began it as a show of brute force and Edward I (1272–1307) completed it. William's Caen stone White Tower, built within old Roman walls, was an excellent defence: It was 27m (90ft) high, with walls 4.5m (15ft) thick, and space for soldiers, servants and nobles. Henry III began the Inner Wall, the moat, his own watergate—and the royal zoo. Edward I completed the Inner Wall, built the Outer Wall, several towers and Traitor's Gate, and moved the mint and Crown Jewels here.

Portrait of a Yeoman or Beefeater (far left), the traditional guard of the Tower of London. The Tower of London (left) illuminated at night as seen across the Thames. Traitor's Gate (right), so called because of the number of prisoners accused of treason who have passed through it. Armoury on display in the Tower of London (below left). A famous Tower of London raven (below right)

Wonder and horror Stephen (1135–54) was the first king to live here, James I (1603–25) the last. From here Edward I went in procession to his coronation and Henry VIII paraded through the city bedecked in cloth of gold. Here the Barons seized the Tower to force King John to put his seal to the Magna Carta in 1215; and here two princes were murdered while their uncle was being crowned Richard III. Since 1485 it has been guarded by Yeoman Warders or 'Beefeaters'.

Centuries of history The Tower has been palace, fortress, state prison and execution site and its gates are still locked every night. If the history is overwhelming there is help: a good welcome area, jolly guided tours, a serious audio tour and interactive displays that take place in the Bloody and Beauchamp towers.

THE BASICS

www.hrp.org.uk

➕ S5

✉ Tower Hill, EC3

☎ 0844 482 7777

🕐 Mar–end Oct Tue–Sat 9–5.30, Sun–Mon 10–5.30; Nov–end Feb Tue–Sat 9–4.30, Sun–Mon 10–4.30

🍴 Cafés, restaurant

Ⓜ Tower Hill

🚆 Fenchurch Street, London Bridge, Docklands Light Railway (Tower Gateway)

♿ Excellent for Jewel House

💷 Expensive

❓ Free guided tours every 30 min; audio tours

More to See

ALL-HALLOWS-BY-THE-TOWER

www.allhallowsbythetower.org.uk
Begun about 1000, the church has a
Roman pavement, a carving by Grinling
Gibbons and the Undercroft Museum.
➕ R5 ✉ Byward Street, EC3 ☎ 020 7481
2928 🕐 Church Mon–Fri 9–6, Sat–Sun 10–5
🚇 Tower Hill 👋 Charge for audio tour

BANK OF ENGLAND MUSEUM

www.bankofengland.co.uk
Britain's monetary and banking system
since 1694, in Soane's lovely rooms.
➕ Q4 ✉ Bartholomew Lane, EC2 ☎ 020
7601 5545 🕐 Mon–Fri 10–5 🚇 Bank
👋 Free

CHRISTCHURCH SPITALFIELDS

www.christchurchspitalfields.org
Nicholas Hawksmoor's 1750 master-
piece has been finely restored.
➕ S3 ✉ Fournier Street, E1 ☎ No phone
🕐 Tue 11–4, Sun 1–4 🚇 Liverpool Street
👋 Donation

CLOCKMAKERS MUSEUM

www.clockmakers.org
A collection of exquisite timepieces
tick-tocking away, including Thomas
Tompion masterpieces.
➕ P4 ✉ Guildhall Library, Aldermanbury,
EC2 ☎ 020 7332 1868 🕐 Mon–Sat
9.30–4.30 🚇 St. Paul's, Bank 👋 Free

DR. JOHNSON'S HOUSE

www.drjohnsonshouse.org
Dr. Samuel Johnson lived here
between 1749 and 1759 while
compiling his dictionary. The house
was built c1700.
➕ M4 ✉ 17 Gough Square, EC4 ☎ 020
7353 3745 🕐 May–end Sep Mon–Sat
11–5.30; Oct–end Apr Mon–Sat 11–5
🚇 Chancery Lane, Blackfriars 🚉 Blackfriars
👋 Moderate

GUILDHALL ART GALLERY

www.guildhall-art-gallery.org.uk
Two remarkable things to see: the
Guildhall's quirky collection of mostly
British pictures, and part of Roman
London's hugh amphitheatre built in
AD200 and recently rediscovered.
➕ P4 ✉ Guildhall Yard, Gresham Street,
EC2 ☎ 020 7332 3700 🕐 Mon–Sat 10–5,
Sun 12–4 🚇 St. Paul's, Bank 👋 Moderate

Hands-on exhibit at the Bank of England Museum

Samuel Johnson remembered in stained glass

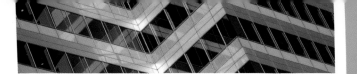

ST. BARTHOLOMEW-THE-GREAT

www.greatstbarts.com

Built in 1123, this is the City's only 12th-century monastic church, and its best surviving piece of large-scale Romanesque architecture.

✚ N3 ✉ West Smithfield, EC1 ☎ 020 7606 5171 🕐 Tue–Fri 8.30–5 (4pm mid-Nov to mid-Feb), Sat 10–30–1.30, Sun 8.30–1, 2.30–8. Sun services 9, 10 (monthly), 11, 6.30 🚇 Barbican, Farringdon, St. Paul's 🚉 Farringdon 🚶 Good 💷 Free, donation encouraged

ST. MARGARET, LOTHBURY

www.stml.org.uk

Wren's church (1686–90) retains its huge carved screen with soaring eagle and carved pulpit tester.

✚ Q4 ✉ Lothbury, EC1 ☎ 020 7606 8330 🕐 Mon–Fri 7–5 🚇 Bank 💷 Donation

TEMPLE CHURCH

www.templechurch.com

Begun about 1160, this private chapel built to a circular plan stands at the heart Temple—two Inns of Court. You can visit the Temple gardens and the 16th-century Middle Temple Hall.

✚ M4 ✉ Inner Temple, EC4 ☎ 020 7353 3470 🕐 Opening times vary, check website. Sun services 🚇 Temple 💷 Donation

TEMPLE OF MITHRAS

Right on the open street, peer at the Roman temple foundations of AD240–250 testifying to the cult of the Persian god Mithras.

✚ P5 ✉ Temple Court, Queen Victoria Street, EC4 🚇 Mansion House, Bank

30 ST. MARY AXE

Rising from a public plaza, this landmark tower, designed by Foster & Partners and affectionately known as the 'gherkin', adds wit to the cluster of tall buildings in London's financial hub. The environmentally progressive building has aerodynamic form encouraging wind flow around its face, together with natural ventilation and light, and energy saving systems.

✚ R4 ✉ 30 St. Mary Axe, EC3 🕐 Not open to the general public 🚇 Bank

St. Margaret, Lothbury

Temple Church

Around the City

To enjoy the City in full swing, do this walk on a weekday. There's a mix of ancient and modern in this 2,000-year-old area of London.

DISTANCE: 2.5km (1.5 miles)   **ALLOW:** 1–2 hours

 START

MONUMENT UNDERGROUND
🚇 Q5 🅜 Monument

 END

BANK UNDERGROUND
🚇 Q4 🅜 Bank

❶ Take the King William Street (south) exit and walk past Monument on your left, and onto London Bridge for views along the river to Tower Bridge. Retrace your steps.

❽ Follow Queen Victoria Street. Turn right into Bow Lane. At the end St. Mary-le-Bow is on the left. Turn right and follow Cheapside right; Bank station is at the bottom of the hill opposite Mansion House.

❷ Go right onto Monument Street to reach Monument. Climb Fish Street Hill to Eastcheap and go right. Cross into Philpot Lane. Lloyd's Building is ahead.

❼ Guildhall is on the right behind St. Lawrence Jewry Church. Facing away from Guildhall (▷ 40), cross Gresham Street through King Street and Queen Street to Queen Victoria Street. Opposite is Temple of Mithras (▷ 41).

❸ At the end, cross Fenchurch Street into Lime Street. Take Lime Street Passage left into Leadenhall Market (▷ 43). Take Whittington Avenue and go right into Leadenhall Street.

❻ At lights cross into Threadneedle Street. Pass the statue of US philanthropist George Peabody on the left. Turn right down Bartholomew Lane past the Bank of England (▷ 40). At the end go left along Lothbury and into Gresham Street.

❹ Carry on to reach the Lloyds Building. Cross the road and go left down St. Mary Axe to 30 St. Mary Axe (the 'Gherkin') on your right. Turn left into Undershaft Square.

❺ Turn right to St. Helen Bishopsgate church. Continue round square to the left and onto Bishopsgate.

Shopping

LEADENHALL MARKET

A surprising City treat housed under Horace Jones's 1880s arcades, with quality butchers, cheesemongers, fishmongers and pubs.

🚇 R4 ✉ Leadenhall, EC3 🕐 Mon–Fri 7–4 🚇 Bank, Monument

PETTICOAT LANE

Look for clothing at bargain prices—especially fabrics and leather.

🚇 S4 ✉ Middlesex and Wentworth streets, E1 🕐 Mon 8–2, Tue–Fri 8–4, Sun 9–2 🚇 Liverpool Street, Aldgate

ROYAL EXCHANGE

William Tite's City landmark is now a beautiful upscale shopping mall, plus bars.

🚇 Q4 ✉ Bank, EC3 🕐 Mon–Fri, times vary from shop to shop 🚇 Bank

SPITALFIELDS MARKET

Crafts and an array of food outlets from crêpes and sushi to tandoori. Organic section Friday and Sunday.

🚇 S3 ✉ Commercial Street, E1 🕐 Mon–Fri 11–3, Sun 9.30–5 🚇 Liverpool Street

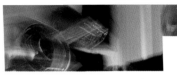

Entertainment and Nightlife

BARBICAN CENTRE THEATRE

www.barbican.org.uk
Currently an exciting mix of domestic and international companies play seasons here.

🚇 R3 ✉ Barbican Centre, Silk Street, EC2 ☎ 020 7638 8891 🚇 Barbican

BARBICAN CONCERT HALL

www.barbican.org.uk.
A 2,000-seat concert hall, home of the London Symphony Orchestra and the English Chamber Orchestra. Also visited by top-notch touring orchestras.

🚇 R3 ✉ Barbican Centre, Silk Street, EC2 ☎ 020 7638 8891; range of good ticket deals 🚇 Barbican

BROADGATE CENTRE

This circular amphitheatre provides a schedule of summer entertainment and a winter ice rink surrounded by chic wine bars, restaurants and a variety of shops.

🚇 R3 ✉ Broadgate Circus, Eldon Street, EC2 ☎ 020 7505 4068 🚇 Liverpool Street

FABRIC

www.fabriclondon.com
This fabulously cool superclub is known for its music blasted out in three rooms and is hugely popular.

🚇 N3 ✉ 77a Charterhouse Street, EC1 ☎ 020 7336 8898 🚇 Farringdon

TURNMILLS

www.turnmills.co.uk
Turnmills hosts some of the world's biggest house music DJs every week and has a 24-hour entertainment licence. There are lots of bars in the adjoining streets, too.

🚇 M3 ✉ 63b Clerkenwell Road, EC1 ☎ 020 7250 3409 🚇 Farringdon

MUSIC EVERYWHERE!

London is full of music. At lunchtime, the best places are churches, where concerts are usually free. Try St. Anne and St. Agnes, and St. Olave's in the City; St. James's, Piccadilly; and St. Martin-in-the-Fields in Trafalgar Square. St. Paul's Cathedral has choral evensong at 5pm Monday to Saturday, 3.15 on Sunday. Look for concerts in historic houses, museums and galleries, especially during the City of London Festival (July). On summer evenings music is played outside in the Embankment Gardens or at Kenwood House (▷ 100).

Restaurants

PRICES

Prices are approximate, based on a 3-course meal for one person.

£££ over £60
££ £30–£60
£ under £30

BEVIS MONKS RESTAURANT (££)

A most stylish kosher restaurant next to the 18th-century synagogue. Israeli and other wines.
R4 ✉ Bevis Monks, EC3 ☎ 020 7283 2220 ⏰ Mon–Fri lunch, Mon–Thu dinner Ⓜ Aldgate

CICADA (£)

Popular minimalist bar/ restaurant that attracts a stylish crowd who create a fun atmosphere.
N3 ✉ 132–136 St. John Street, EC1 ☎ 020 7608 1550 ⏰ Mon–Fri 12–11, Sat 6–11 Ⓜ Farringdon

CLUB GASCON (£££)

Unusual, robust dishes from Gascony; good for that special dinner. Reserve well in advance.
N3 ✉ 57 West Smithfield, EC1 ☎ 020 7796 0600 ⏰ Mon–Fri lunch, Mon–Sat dinner Ⓜ Barbican, Farringdon

THE EAGLE (£)

The original London new-wave pub (1991) serves robust, Mediterranean food to a noisy, full house.
M3 ✉ 159 Farringdon Road, EC1 ☎ 020 7837 1353 ⏰ Mon–Sat 12–11, Sun 12–5 Ⓜ Farringdon

FLANEUR FOOD HALL (££)

Witty interior design in a spacious converted warehouse. Modern Mediterranean food composed with super-fresh ingredients.
M3 ✉ 41 Farringdon Road, EC1 ☎ 020 7404 4422 ⏰ Mon–Sat 9am–10pm Ⓜ Farringdon

HAZ (£)

www.hazrestaurant.co.uk
Delicious Persian and Turkish food in a sleek canteen setting.
R4 ✉ 9 Cutler Street, E1 ☎ 020 7929 7923 ⏰ 11am–11.30pm daily Ⓜ Liverpool Street

K–10 (£)

www.k10.net
Head down to the lounge basement for the high tech Kaiten-sushi bar, probably London's best.
Q4 ✉ Shop 5, Northern Line Arcade, EC2 ☎ 020 7614 9910 ⏰ Mon–Fri 7.30am–4pm Ⓜ Moorgate

VEGETARIAN EATING

Vegetarians are well-catered to in London. Most restaurants offer a range of non-meat and nonfish meals, while Indian cooking is famed for its imaginative vegetable and pulse dishes. If fish remains an option, the capital has a wide range on offer.

PEASANT (£)

www.thepeasant.co.uk
Excellent innovative Mediterranean food in a pub touched with the wand of a design-conscious foodie.
N3 ✉ 240 St. John Street, EC1 ☎ 020 7336 7726 ⏰ Pub: Mon–Fri 12–11, Sat 6pm–11pm, Sun 12–10.30. Restaurant: Mon–Fri 12–3, 6–11, Sat 6pm–11pm, Sun 12–3 Ⓜ Farringdon

THE PLACE BELOW (£)

www.theplacebelow.co.uk
Exceptional vegetarian food in an ancient Norman church crypt in the heart of the City.
P4 ✉ St. Mary-le-Bow, Cheapside, EC2 ☎ 020 7329 0789 ⏰ Mon–Fri breakfast and lunch Ⓜ Monument

RHODES TWENTY FOUR (£££)

Gary Rhodes provides the ulitmate City experience: fine British food and amazing City views.
Q4 ✉ 24th floor, Tower 42, Old Broad Street, EC2 ☎ 020 7877 7703 ⏰ Mon–Fri 12–2.30, 6–9 Ⓜ Liverpool Street

ST. JOHN (££)

www.stjohnrestaurant.com
Robust dishes ranging from rabbit to oxtails to serious puddings, which include such delights as lemon possett.
N3 ✉ 26 St. John Street, EC1 ☎ 020 7251 0848 ⏰ Mon–Fri 12–3, Mon–Sat 6pm–11pm Ⓜ Farringdon

London expanded out of its City walls due to the great trade boom of the 18th century, when aristocrats and developers lavished money on elegant squares and terraces. Today, this elegant area is home to many fascinating museums as well.

Sights	**48–53**	Top 25	**TOP 25**
Shopping	**54–55**	British Museum ▷ **48**	
Entertainment and Nightlife	**56**	Sir John Soane's Museum ▷ **50**	
Restaurants	**57–58**	Somerset House ▷ **51**	

Thomas Coram Foundation
(The Foundling Museum)

Hunter Street
Handel Street
Herbrand Street
Marchmont Street
Brunswick Square
Coram's Fields

Charles Dickens Museum

Burgh Place
Doughty Mews
Gough Street
Elm Street

GRAY'S INN ROAD

WOBURN PLACE
Coram Street
Bernard Street
Brunswick Shopping Centre
LANSDOWNE
GUILFORD STREET
GUILFORD
GRENVILLE STREET
B502
Colonnade
National Hospital for Sick Children (Great Ormond St)
Millman Street
Roger Street
Doughty Street
John's Mews
Northington Street

London Weather Centre

RUSSELL
A4200
Russell Square
National Hospital for Neurology & Neurosurgery
Great Ormond Street
Orde Hall Street
Lamb's Conduit Street
Rugby Street
Emerald Street
Dombey Street
James Street
Bedford Row
Jockey's Fields

PLACE
RUSSELL
SQUARE
Russell Square
Queen Square
Royal London Homeopathic Hospital
Boswell Street
New North Street
THEOBALD'S ROAD
Princeton Street
Sandland Street

Gray's Inn
Inns of Court & School of Law
Gray's Inn Square
South Square

BLOOMSBURY
SOUTHAMPTON ROW
Old Gloucester Street
Conway Hall
Red Lion Square
Eagle Street
Great Russell Street
A5200

Montague Street
Bedford Place
WAY
VERNON PLACE
DAVE PROCTER STREET
Carlton Street

British Museum

HOLBORN
HIGH HOLBORN
CHANCERY LANE

The Cartoon Museum
Coptic Street
Gilbert Place
Little Russell Street
BLOOMSBURY
SOUTHAMPTON
Barter Street
Newton Street
Sir John Soane's Museum
Whetstone Park
Remnant Street
Lincoln's Inn Fields
Newman's Row
Buildings

New Oxford Street
New Oxford Street
Holborn
HOLBORN
Lincoln's Inn
Lincoln's Inn
Lincoln's Inn
Lincoln's Row
New Square

A40
OXFORD ST
A400
AVENUE
ST GILES HIGH ST
HIGH ST
SHAFTESBURY AVENUE
ENDELL
High Holborn
Drury Lane
Shelton Street
Mackin Street
Parker Street
QUEEN ST
B402
KINGSWAY
GT
Hunterian Museum
Old Curiosity Shop
Lincoln's
Sardinia Street
Portugal Street
Lincoln's Row
Serle Street
Carey Street
Royal College of Surgeons

ST GILES
Oasis Sports Centre
Betterton Street
Arne Street
Wild Street
New Connaught Rooms
St Clement's Lane
Clement's
Carey Street
Royal Courts of Justice

HIGH ST
Compton Street
Neal's Yard
Shorts Gardens
Earlham Street
Short's Gardens
Langley Street
ENDELL STREET
ACRE
Bow Street
Drury Lane
Inn
London School of Economics & Political Science
Clement's Inn
STRAND A4

UPPER ST MARTIN'S LANE
Mercer Street
Shelton Street
Floral Street
Royal Opera House
Russell Street
Kean Street
Catherine Street
ALDWYCH
Bush House (BBC)
Australia House
AA
St Clement Danes
Essex Street
Milford Lane

Photographers' Gallery
Covent Garden
LONG ACRE
Covent Garden Piazza
King St
Piazza
Tavistock St
London Transport Museum
Wellington St
Catherine St
India House
AA
St Mary-le-Strand
Roman Bath
Surrey Street
Arundel Street
Temple Place
Temple

ST MARTIN'S LANE
New Row
Garrick St
Bedfordbury
St Paul's Church
St Peter's Hospital
Maiden Lane
STRAND
Exeter St
Courtauld Institute of Art
Somerset House
King's College
Hermitage Rooms
EMBANKMENT

New Row
Bedford St
Chandos Place
William IV Street
STRAND
Savoy Street
Savoy Hill
Gilbert Collection

Royal Society of Arts
Proud Galleries
Adam Street
Savoy Place
WATERLOO BRIDGE

VICTORIA
WATERLOO BRIDGE
Savoy Pier
Embankment Pier

Victoria Embankment Gardens
Cleopatra's Needle

Thames

GOLDEN JUBILEE BRIDGE

K   L

British Museum

HIGHLIGHTS

- Enlightenment Gallery
- Oriental antiquities
- African Galleries
- Rosetta Stone
- Living and Dying Gallery
- Elgin Marbles
- Assyrian and Egyptian rooms
- The King's Library
- Norman Foster's Great Court redevelopment

TIPS

- Get your bearings in the Great Court.
- Take an Eye Opener tour.
- Do the Hands-On object handling.
- Rent an audio guide.

It's fun to choose your own seven wonders of the world in the British Museum. It's likely the bronzes from the Indian Chola dynasty and the lion-filled reliefs that once lined an Assyrian palace will be on the list.

Physician founder Sir Hans Sloane, after whom Sloane Square is named, was a fashionable London physician, 'interested in the whole of human knowledge' and an avid collector of everything from plants to prints. When he died in 1753 at age 92 he left his collection of more than 80,000 objects to the nation on condition that it was given a permanent home. Thus began the British Museum, opened in 1759 in a 17th-century mansion, Britain's first public museum and now its largest, covering 5.5ha (13.5 acres).

One of the many obsorbing galleries the British Museum has to offer (left). Taking front-stage, the Great Court is like the mother ship watching over the British Museum (right)

It grew and grew Kings George II, III and IV made magnificent gifts, as did other monarchs, to Sloane's collection. These, with the Townley and Elgin Marbles, burst the building's seams and the architect Robert Smirke designed a grand new museum, completed by his son, Sydney, in 1857. Even so, because the booty from expeditions and excavations poured in continuously, the Natural History collections went to South Kensington (▷ 86). With the departure of the British Library (▷ 99) to St. Pancras in 1998, the Great Court has been redeveloped and the King's Library transformed into a gallery about the Enlightenment.

A right way A good way to explore is to pick up a plan in the Great Court, see what special events are on, choose at the most three rooms to see, and then set off to find them.

THE BASICS

www.thebritishmuseum.ac.uk

⊞ J3

✉ Great Russell Street, WC1 (another entrance in Montague Place)

☎ 020 7323 8000

🕐 Daily 10–5.30 (galleries). Great Court Mon–Wed, Sun 9–6, Thu–Sat 9am–11pm

🍴 Restaurant, cafés

Ⓔ Holborn, Tottenham Court Road

Ⓖ Very good

🎟 Free except for some temporary exhibitions, tours and late openings

❓ Full educational schedule

Sir John Soane's Museum

Some of the fascinating items concealed in Sir John Soane's Museum

THE BASICS

www.soane.org
🚼 L4
✉ 13 Lincoln's Inn Fields, WC2
☎ 020 7405 2107
🕐 Tue–Sat 10–5 (also 1st Tue of month 6–9pm); closed 24–26 Dec, 1 Jan, Good Fri
🚇 Holborn, Chancery Lane (closed Sun)
🚆 Farringdon
💷 Free (donation)
❓ Guided tours Sat 2.30

HIGHLIGHTS

● *The Rake's Progress, The Election*, Hogarth
● Sarcophagus of Seti I
● Lawrence's portrait of Soane
● Monk's Parlour

TIPS

● Unsuitable for children.
● Candlelight evening openings, monthly.
● Tours on Saturday.

As you move about the gloriously over-furnished rooms of Soane's two houses and into the calm upstairs drawing room, his presence is so strong you feel you would not be surprised if he were there to greet you.

The architect This double treasure-house in leafy Lincoln's Inn Fields, central London's largest square, is where the neoclassical architect Sir John Soane lived. First he designed No. 12 and lived there from 1792. Then he bought No. 13 next door, rebuilt it with cunningly proportioned rooms, and lived there from 1813 until his death in 1837. Meanwhile, he also designed Holy Trinity church on Marylebone Road (1824–48), and parts of the Treasury, Whitehall. His model for his masterpiece, the (destroyed) Bank of England, is here (re-created rooms now form the bank's museum ▷ 40). No. 14 is now an area for Adam Studies.

The collector Soane was an avid collector. He found that every art object could inspire his work, so his rooms were a visual reference library. Hogarth's paintings unfold from the walls in layers. There are so many sculptures, paintings and antiquities that unless you keep your eyes peeled you will miss a Watteau drawing or something better.

The ghost of Soane Sir John's ingenious designs pervade every room, as do the stories of his passion for collecting. For example, when an Egyptian sarcophagus arrived, he gave a three-day party in its recognition of its prestige.

The stunning exterior is a mere taster of the treasures that await inside Somerset House

Somerset House

Somerset House was transformed from a lavish but forgotten building into a riverside palace. Spend a day here and enjoy French Impressionist masterpieces, English silver and some of Russian art.

Palatial home A majestic, triple-arch gateway leads from the Strand into Sir William Chamber's English Palladian government offices (1776–86). Within the gateway, the Courtauld Collection is housed in rooms lavishly decorated for the Royal Academy, before its move to Piccadilly. Ahead, the great courtyard has fountains, a theatre, an ice-rink and café tables, according to the season. The rooms overlooking the Thames contain a restaurant, café and two special interest treats: the Gilbert Collection and the Hermitage Rooms.

Courtauld Gallery A stunning collection of French Impressionist paintings—Renoir, Cezanne, van Gogh, Gaugin, Manet—collected by the industrialist Samuel Courtauld. The art feast also has Italian Renaissance panels, Rubens canvases and Ben Nicholsons.

Gilbert Collection Arthur Gilbert, born in London, made his fortune in California and spent it on art in three fields: Roman and Florentine mosaics, gold and silverware and 18th-century gold snuff boxes. Then he gave it all to his home town.

Hermitage Rooms An outpost of the State Hermitage Museum in St. Petersburg, the 500 or so exhibits selected from its astoundingly rich collection change regularly.

THE BASICS

www.somersethouse.org.uk
+ L5
⊠ Somerset House, Strand, WC2
☎ 020 7845 4600
🕐 Daily 10–6; extended hours for Courtyard, River Terrace and restaurant.
🍴 Cafés, restaurant
Ⓣ Temple (closed Sun)
🚇 Blackfriars, Charing Cross
♿ Excellent
📋 Somerset House free; collections moderate, Mon 10–2 free

HIGHLIGHTS

Courtauld Collection:
● The Fridart Collection
● *Bar at the Folies-Bergere*, Manet
● Rubens paintings
● *The Trinity*, Botticelli
Gilbert Collection:
● Micro-mosaic table top with views of Rome
● Silver ewer, Paul de Lamerie
● 18th-century enamel snuff boxes

More to See

CLEOPATRA'S NEEDLE
The 26m (86ft) pink-granite obelisk was made in 1450BC and records the triumphs of Rameses the Great.
K6 ⊠ Victoria Embankment, WC2 Ⓡ Embankment, Charing Cross 🎟 Free

COVENT GARDEN PIAZZA
London's first square was laid out in the 1630s by architect Inigo Jones. It later became a fruit and vegetable market. Today, cleaned up, it mixes retail with entertainment.
K5 Ⓡ Covent Garden

DICKENS' HOUSE MUSEUM
www.dickensmuseum.com
The house where Dickens wrote Nicholas Nickleby and Oliver Twist.
L2 ⊠ 48 Doughty Street, WC1 ☎ 020 7405 2127 🕐 Mon–Sat 10–5, Sun 11–5 Ⓡ Russell Square 🎟 Moderate

EROS
Alfred Gilbert's memorial (1893) to the philanthropic 7th Earl of Shaftesbury (1801–85) actually portrays the Angel of Christian Charity, not Eros.

H5 ⊠ Piccadilly Circus, W1 Ⓡ Piccadilly Circus

FOUNDLING MUSEUM
www.foundlingmuseum.org.uk
When Thomas Coran founded a hospice for abandoned children in 1739, Handel and Hogarth helped raise funds. Magnificent building and art.
K2 ⊠ 40 Brunswick Square, WC1 ☎ 020 7841 3600 🕐 Tue–Sat 10–6, Sun 12–6 Ⓡ Russell Square 🎟 Moderate

HANDEL HOUSE MUSEUM
www.handelhouse.org
Anyone who plays a muscial instrument or sings 'The Messiah' should not miss a visit to the composer's London home from 1723 until 1759.
G5 ⊠ 25 Brook Street, W1 ☎ 020 7495 1685 🕐 Tue–Wed, Fri–Sat 10–6, Thu 10–8, Sun 12–6 Ⓡ Bond Street 🎟 Moderate

HUNTERIAN MUSEUM
www.rcseng.ac.uk
Brilliantly ghoulish exhibits from the anotomical collection of John Hunter.
L4 ⊠ Royal College of Surgeons,

A harpsichord, Handel House

Eros, Piccadilly Circus

Lincoln's Inn Fields, WC2 ☎ 020 7869 6560
🕐 Tue–Sat 10–5 🚇 Holborn 🎟 Free

LONDON TRANSPORT MUSEUM
www.ltmuseum.co.uk
After a £22 million redesign, this
museum has several high-tech new
galleries giving information on London's
communities, as well as the past and
future of the city's transport system.
✚ K5 ✉ Covent Garden Piazza, WC2
☎ 020 7379 6344 🕐 Sat–Thu 10–6, Fri
11–9 🍴 Café 🚇 Covent Garden
🚆 Charing Cross 🎟 Moderate

PERCIVAL DAVID FOUNDATION OF CHINESE ART
www.pdfmuseum.org.uk
Sublime Chinese ceramics.
✚ J2 ✉ 53 Gordon Square, WC1 ☎ 020
7387 3909 🕐 Mon–Fri 10–12.30, 1.30–5
🚇 Russell Square 🎟 Free

PETRIE MUSEUM
www.petrie.ucl.ac.uk
The ancient spoils of many egyptolo-
gists' explorations are on display at the
hard-to-find Petrie Museum (it's close
to the rear of the British Museum).
✚ J2 ✉ Univeristy College London, Malet
Place, WC1E ☎ 020 7679 2884 🕐 Tue–Fri
1–5, Sat 10–1 🚇 Euston Square 🎟 Free

PHOTOGRAPHERS' GALLERY
www.photographersgallery.org.uk
Contemporary photos displayed in
the heart of London.
✚ J5 ✉ 5–8 Great Newport Street, WC2
☎ 020 7831 1772 🕐 Mon–Sat 11–6, Sun
12–6 🚇 Leicester Square 🎟 Free

ROYAL ACADEMY OF ARTS
www.royalacademy.org.uk
Major art shows, plus the annual
Summer Exhibition. Don't miss
rooftop Sackler Galleries.
✚ H5 ✉ Burlington House, Piccadilly, W1
☎ 020 7300 8000 🕐 Sat–Thu 10–6, Fri
10–10 🍴 Restaurant, café 🚇 Green Park,
Piccadilly 🎟 Expensive

RUSSELL SQUARE
Lawns, trees and a good café near
the British Museum.
✚ K3 ✉ WC1 🕐 Daily 7–dusk 🍴 Café
🚇 Russell Square 🎟 Free

The black-tiled exterior of the Photographers' Gallery

There's always lots going on at the Royal Academy of Arts

Shopping

ANDERSON & SHEPPARD

One of the best British tailors, Anderson's was established in 1906 serving the rich and famous. Hand-crafted suits by expert tailors result in very high prices.

⊞ G5 ✉ 32 Old Burlington Street, W1S ☎ 020 7734 1420 🚇 Piccadilly Circus, Oxford Circus

ARAM DESIGNS LTD

Aram's international modern designs are displayed on five floors. Stock includes furniture, lighting and glass.

⊞ K4 ✉ 110 Drury Lane, WC2 ☎ 020 7557 7557 🚇 Covent Garden

BERNARD QUARITCH

It is best to make an appointment to come to this, the most splendid and serious of the city's antiquarian bookshops.

⊞ H5 ✉ 5 Lower John Street, W1 ☎ 020 7734 2983 🚇 Piccadilly Circus

BONHAM'S

This auction house gains in reputation every year. Especially good for specialist sales. Secondary salesroom in Chelsea.

⊞ G5 ✉ 101 New Bond Street, W1 ☎ 020 7447 7447 🚇 Bond Street

BROWN'S

This boutique has long led the fashion pack, offering chic designs at grown-up prices.

⊞ F4 ✉ 23–27 South Molton Street, W1 ☎ 020 7514 0000 🚇 Bond Street

CARLUCCIO'S

This designer deli chain stocks only the most refined goods, such as truffle oil, black pasta and balsamic vinegar.

⊞ K4 ✉ Garrick Street, WC2E ☎ 020 7836 0990 🚇 Covent Garden

CONTEMPORARY APPLIED ARTS

The best central London gathering of quality contemporary crafts.

⊞ J3 ✉ 2 Percy Street, W1 ☎ 020 7436 2344 🚇 Goodge Street

THE FINE ART SOCIETY

This is one of the oldest and friendliest galleries in town.

⊞ G5 ✉ 148 New Bond Street, W1 ☎ 020 7629 5116 🚇 Bond Street

BUYING AT AUCTION

Watching an auction is one thing; buying is quite another. At the presale viewing, inspect any lot you may bid for and check its description and estimated sale price in the catalogue. If you cannot attend the sale, leave a bid; if you can, decide on your maximum bid and do not go above it! Bid by lifting your hand up high. If successful, pay and collect after the sale, or arrange for delivery.

FORBIDDEN PLANET

Come here for an amazing selection of fantasy, horror, science fiction; plus comic books.

⊞ J4 ✉ 179 Shaftesbury Avenue, WC2 ☎ 020 7420 3666 🚇 Tottenham Court Road

GRAYS ANTIQUE MARKET

High-quality goods ranging from pictures to silver are sold at around 170 stands.

⊞ F5 ✉ 1–7 Davies Mews and 58 Davies Street, W1 ☎ 020 7629 7034 🚇 Bond Street

HEAL'S

A frontrunner of the Arts and Crafts movement in the 1920s, Heal's particularly specializes in timeless contemporary furniture.

⊞ J3 ✉ 196 Tottenham Court Road, W1 ☎ 020 7636 1666 🚇 Goodge Street

JIGSAW

Well-cut, romantic clothes with style and character at reasonable prices.

⊞ G5 ✉ 126–127 New Bond Street, W1 ☎ 020 7491 4484 🚇 Bond Street

JOHN LEWIS

Its slogan, 'never knowingly undersold', inspires a confidence that prices are solidly fair.

⊞ G4 ✉ Oxford Street, W1 ☎ 020 7629 7711 🚇 Oxford Circus

KOH SAMUI

Many boutiques in London

stock top British designers but Koh Samui has established names as well as the names of the future. This Covent Garden shop displays a wealth of new talent displayed on its racks and shelves.

⊕ J4 ✉ 66–67 Monmouth Street, WC2 ☎ 020 7240 4280 Ⓠ Covent Garden, Leicester Square

LIBERTY

Offering everything from sumptuous fabrics to china and glass, this shop's quality is characterized by exoticism and cutting-edge fashion mixed with an Arts and Crafts heritage all brought together in a beautiful mock-Tudor building.

⊕ G4 ✉ Great Marlbourough Street, W1 ☎ 020 7734 1234 Ⓠ Oxford Circus

MASSIMO DUTTI

Beautiful clothes in a deligfhtful shop, and an added bonus, they're all for reasonable prices.

⊕ G4 ✉ 156 Regent Street, W1 ☎ 020 7851 1280 Ⓠ Oxford Circus

NEAL'S YARD DAIRY

This shop is a temple to the British cheese, where more than 50 varieties from small farms in Britain are ripened to perfection. In business since 1979.

⊕ K4 ✉ 17 Shorts Gardens, WC2 ☎ 020 7240 5700 Ⓠ Covent Garden

NEAL'S YARD REMEDIES

Among Covent Garden's many quality health and beauty shops, this one has been committed to natural ingredients for more than 20 years.

⊕ K4 ✉ 15 Neal's Yard, WC2 ☎ 020 7379 7222 Ⓠ Covent Garden

THE SANCTUARY

Stock up on lotions, potions, scrubs and oils at this Covent Garden spa, all promoting Spa perfect skin.

⊕ K5 ✉ 12 Floral Street, WC2E ☎ 0870 770 3350 Ⓠ Covent Garden

SELFRIDGES

A rival to Harvey Nichols (▷ 90) for daylong girlie retail therapy. Don't miss the superb food hall.

⊕ F4 ✉ 400 Oxford Street, W1 ☎ 0800 123 400 Ⓠ Oxford Circus

BOOKSHOP CAFÉS

To browse in a bookshop with its own in-house café, try Borders Books, Music and Café (✉ 203 Oxford Street, W1 ☎ 020 7292 1600); their Charing Cross Road branch also has a café. Central London branches of Books Etc with cafés include those on Charing Cross Road, Oxford Street and Piccadilly. Waterstone's superstore on Piccadilly has a café, juice bar and a restaurant with great views.

SOTHEBY'S

The world's largest auction house. A rabbit warren of sale rooms with objects of all kinds on display. The 'Colonnade' sales are less expensive.

⊕ G5 ✉ 34 New Bond Street, W1 ☎ 020 7293 5000 Ⓠ Bond Street

SPINK & SON

Best known for their coins, medals, stamps and banknotes.

⊕ K3 ✉ 69 Southampton Row, WC1 ☎ 020 7563 4000 Ⓠ Holborn

STANFORDS

London's largest selection of maps of countries, cities and even very small towns around the world, plus travel books.

⊕ K5 ✉ 12–14 Long Acre, WC2 ☎ 020 7836 1321 Ⓠ Covent Garden

VILLANDRY

Quality 'foodstore' with best buys taking in French and English cheeses, great breads, olive oil and much more.

⊕ G3 ✉ 170 Great Portland Street, W1N ☎ 020 7631 3131 Ⓠ Great Portland Street

ZWEMMER ARTS BOOKSHOP

Art books fill three areas of this bookshop divided by category. Here, fine art is upstairs, decorative art and architecture downstairs.

⊕ K5 ✉ 24 Litchfield Street, WC2 ☎ 020 7240 4158 Ⓠ Leicester Square

Entertainment and Nightlife

THE BORDERLINE
www.meanfiddler.com
The hottest indie and rock bands strut their stuff at the venerable Borderline club in the West End.
🟥 J4 ✉ Orange Yard, Manette Street, W1D ☎ 020 7734 5547 🄰 Tottenham Court Road

THE COLISEUM
www.eno.org
The renovated home to the English National Opera, which is known for exciting and innovative productions.
🟥 J5 ✉ St. Martin's Lane, WC2 ☎ 0871 911 0200 🄰 Leicester Square

DONMAR WAREHOUSE
www.donmarwarehouse.com
Avant-garde productions for the adventurous.
🟥 J4 ✉ 41 Earlham Street, WC2H ☎ 0870 060 6624 🄰 Covent Garden

THE END
www.end club.com
Varied music in a well-designed West End club with super-cool AKA bar above.
🟥 K4 ✉ 18a West Central Street, WC1 ☎ 020 7419 9199 🄰 Holborn, Tottenham Court Road

GUANABARA
www.guanabara.co.uk
Grab a *caipirinha* and salsa onto the dance floor at this Brazilian-theme venue. Tables must be booked in advance.
🟥 K4 ✉ Parker Street,

WC2B ☎ 020 7242 8600 🄰 Covent Garden

JAZZ AFTER DARK
www.jazzafterdark.co.uk
Jazz and blues attracts a keen young crowd. Good cocktails, simple food.
🟥 J5 ✉ 9 Greek Street, W1 ☎ 020 7734 0545 🄰 Leicester Square

PIZZA EXPRESS JAZZ CLUB
www.pizzaexpress.com
Quality pizzas and great, often mainstream, jazz in this friendly Soho cellar. Other branches have live jazz, too.
🟥 J5 ✉ 10 Dean Street, W1 ☎ 020 7439 8722 🄰 Tottenham Court Road

ROYAL OPERA HOUSE
www.royaloperahouse.org.uk
Lavish setting for grand opera, daytime free entertainment and the home of the Royal Ballet.
🟥 K4 ✉ Bow Street, Covent Garden, WC2 ☎ 020 7304 4000 🄰 Covent Garden

---

ALL THAT JAZZ
London boasts a great concentration of world-class jazz musicians, both homegrown and foreign, traditional and contemporary. Evening and late-night gigs cover rock, roots, rhythm and blues and more, many in pubs. For a list of venues, check *Time Out*. Also check out the latest information on jazz on www.jazznights.co.uk

SALSA!
www.barsalsa.info
Dance the night away after a class held in the bar, and eat some tasty Latin American food as you practise.
🟥 J5 ✉ 96 Charing Cross Road, WC2 ☎ 020 7379 3277 🄰 Tottenham Court Road

SMOLLENSKY'S ON THE STRAND
www.smollenskys.co.uk
Pianist on week nights, jazz on Sunday nights, at this traditional American bar-restaurant.
🟥 K5 ✉ 105 The Strand, WC2 ☎ 020 7497 2101 🄰 Charing Cross

THEATRE ROYAL DRURY LANE
The present theatre, built in 1812, stages mostly musicals. And there are ghosts—the Man in Grey is said to walk around the Upper Circle.
🟥 K5 ✉ Catherine Street, WC2 ☎ 0870 890 1109 🄰 Covent Garden

WIGMORE HALL
www.wigmore-hall.co.uk
One of London's most beautiful and congenial settings for listening to recitals and chamber music, especially for Sunday concerts. The hall was built in 1901 as a recital hall for Bechstein Pianos, it has perfect accoustics.
🟥 F4 ✉ 36 Wigmore Street, W1 ☎ 020 7935 2141 🄰 Bond Street

Restaurants

COVENT GARDEN TO BLOOMSBURY

RESTAURANTS

PRICES

Prices are approximate, based on a 3-course meal for one person.

£££   over £60
££   £30–£60
££   under £30

THE ADMIRALTY (££)

www.somersethouse.org.uk
Oliver Peyton's modern continental dishes in a stunning site.
⊞ L5 ✉ Somerset House, WC2 ☎ 020 7845 4646 ◷ Mon–Fri 12–2.30, 6–10.30, Sat 12–4, 6–10.30, Sun 12–4 Ⓢ Temple

BENARES (££)

www.benaresrestaurant.com
Atul Kochhar serves up serious Indian dishes including unusual recipes.
⊞ G5 ✉ 12 Berkeley House, Berkeley Square, W1 ☎ 020 7629 8886 ◷ Daily 12–2.30, Mon–Sat 5.30–11, Sun 6–10.30 Ⓢ Green Park

CHRISTOPHER'S (£££)

www.christophersgrill.com
One of London's best for a genuine American brunch, in a most beautiful Victorian town house dining room.
⊞ K5 ✉ 18 Wellington Street, WC2 ☎ 020 7240 4222 ◷ Mon–Fri 7–10, 12–3, 5–11.30, Sat 11.30–3.30, 5–11.30, Sun 11.30–3.30, 5–10.30 Ⓢ Covent Garden

DETROIT (£)

www.detroit-bar.com
Retro decor and a quality barman at this established Covent Garden bar-restaurant.
⊞ K4 ✉ 35 Earlham Street, WC2 ☎ 020 7240 2662 ◷ Lunch and dinner Ⓢ Leicester Square

EAT-THAI.NET (££)

www.et-thai.net
Enjoy classic Thai dishes at this quiet, stylish restaurant with Thai furnishings and Thai modern art, just behind Oxford Street.
⊞ F4 ✉ 22 St. Christopher's Place, W1U ☎ 020 7486 0777 ◷ Daily 12–10.30 Ⓢ Bond Street

GABY'S (£)

Inspired by a New York Jewish diner, this is no-nonsense hearty good-value eating.
⊞ J5 ✉ 30 Charing Cross Road, WC2 ☎ 020 7836 4233 ◷ Mon–Sat 11am–midnight, Sun 12–10pm Ⓢ Leicester Square

THE BILL

When the bill (check) arrives, read it carefully as a service charge (usually 10–15 per cent) and sometimes cover charges (approximately £2 per person) may be added. Check whether VAT and coffee are also included, and order tap water if you do not want to pay for bottled. A good-value menu can transform into a hefty bill. You are not obliged to leave a tip if service is added even if the credit card slip is left open.

HIBISCUS (£££)

www.hibiscusrestaurant.co.uk
Award-winning chef Claude Bosi has relocated his stunning French restaurant from Ludlow to London. Expect artful, inventive dishes at a price.
⊞ G5 ✉ 29 Maddox Street, W1S ☎ 020 7629 2999 ◷ Mon–Fri 12–2.30, 6.30–10 Ⓢ Oxford Circus

IMLI (££)

www.imli.co.uk
Forget old-fashioned Indian restaurants: light, good-value Indian food is Imli's specialty, served in a bright, airy contemporary dining room.
⊞ H4 ✉ 167–169 Wardour Street, W1F ☎ 020 7287 4243 ◷ Mon–Tue 12–11, Wed–Sat 12–11.30, Sun 12–10 Ⓢ Tottenham Court Road

JOE ALLEN (££)

www.joeallen.co.uk
Dependably convivial and clublike establishment serving healthy American Cal-Ital food. Reservations are essential.
⊞ K5 ✉ 13 Exeter Street, WC2 ☎ 020 7836 0651 ◷ Mon–Fri 8–11.30, noon–12.45am, Sat–Sun 12–11.30 Ⓢ Covent Garden

LOWLANDER (£)

www.lowlander.com
Excellent gastro-bar, well-located for pretheatre sustenance.
⊞ K4 ✉ 36 Drury Lane, WC2 ☎ 020 7379 7446 ◷ Mon–Fri 9am–11pm, Sat–Sun 10am–11pm Ⓢ Covent Garden

MASALA ZONE (££)

www.masalazone.com
From the creators of Chutney Mary and Veeraswamy, both loved for their authentic dishes, comes an informal setting for the distinctive Gujarati meals of western India. Other branches.
H5 ✉ 9 Marshall Street, W1 ☎ 020 7287 9966 🕔 Mon–Fri from noon, Sat–Sun from 12.30 🚇 Oxford Circus

PAUL (£)

www.paul.fr
This stunning patisserie is a branch of its French mother founded in 1889. Sample divine hot chocolate and pastries. Other branches.
K5 ✉ 29 Bedford Street, WC2 ☎ 020 7836 3304 🕔 7.30am–9pm 🚇 Covent Garden

RASA SAMUDRA (£)

www.rasarestaurants.com
Inspired Keralan cooking, one of India's softer styles. Several siblings.
H3 ✉ 6 Dering Street, W1 ☎ 020 7637 0222 🕔 Mon–Sat 12–3, 6–11 🚇 Goodge Street

RULES (££)

www.rules.co.uk
One of London's oldest restaurants, founded in 1798, which serves good traditional English dishes in plush Edwardian rooms.
K5 ✉ 35 Maiden Lane, WC2 ☎ 020 7836 5314

🕔 Mon–Sat 12–11.30, Sun 12–10.30 🚇 Covent Garden

SHOCHU (£)

www.shochulounge.com
Tucked below Roka restaurant serving contemporary Japanese cuisine, this popular bar is named after a Japanese spirit best drunk with fresh fruit juice.
H3 ✉ 37 Charlotte Street, W1 ☎ 020 7580 6464 🕔 Mon 5–12, Tue–Fri 12–12, Sat 5–12, Sun 6–12 🚇 Goodge Street

THE SQUARE (£££)

www.squarerestaurant.com
Impressive modern French food from Philip Howard matched by a chic, but formal Mayfair interior.
G5 ✉ 6 Bruton Street, W1 ☎ 020 7495 7100 🕔 Mon–Fri 12–3, 6.30–10.45, Sat 6.30–10.45, Sun 6.30–10 🚇 Bond Street

SET-PRICE MENUS

Many of London's pricier restaurants offer two set-price menus serving sublime dishes—lower in price at lunchtime. Consider dressing up to try classic Anglo-French cuisine at the exquisite Connaught Grill (E5 ✉ 16 Carlos Place, W1 ☎ 020 7499 7070) or spend an afternoon lunching at Gordon Ramsey's Maze (▷ 92). Most of the star chefs offer these menus including Richard Corrigan and Philip Howard.

WAGAMAMA (£)

www.wagamama.com
Japanese ramen bar near the British Museum. About 20 branches; no reservations.
J4 ✉ 4a Streatham Street, WC1 ☎ 020 7323 9223 🕔 Mon–Sat 12–11, 12–10 🚇 Tottenham Court Road

WILD HONEY (££–£££)

Lunch at this new restaurant is a bargain given the standard of Modern European cooking on display. The wine list is also reasonably priced.
G5 ✉ 12 St. George Street, W1S ☎ 020 7758 9160 🕔 Mon–Sat 12–2.30, 5.30–10.30, Sun 12–3.30, 5.30–9.30 🚇 Oxford Circus, Bond Street

WORLD FOOD CAFÉ (££)

A fresh, modern approach to vegetarian food that features Indian, Mexican, Greek and Turkish influences.
K4 ✉ 14 Neal's Yard, WC2 ☎ 020 7379 0298 🕔 Mon–Fri 11.30–4.30, Sat 11.30–5 🚇 Covent Garden

ZIZZI (££)

Conveniently located close to the British Museum, Zizzi serves moderately priced antipasti, pasta and pizzas straight from the wood-fired oven.
H3 ✉ 33–41 Charlotte Street, W1T ☎ 020 7436 9440 🕔 Daily 12–11.30 🚇 Tottenham Court Road

The political, royal and spiritual heart of London. Here you have royal palaces, the Houses of Parliament, Westminster Abbey, and the parks, mansions and shops that kept courtiers and politicians amused.

Sights	62–75
Walk	76
Shopping	77
Entertainment and Nightlife	79
Restaurants	80

Top 25

Buckingham Palace ▷ **62**
Banqueting House ▷ **64**
Houses of Parliament ▷ **65**
National Gallery ▷ **66**
National Portrait Gallery ▷ **67**
St. James's Park ▷ **68**
Tate Britain ▷ **69**
Thames River Cruise ▷ **70**
Westminster Abbey ▷ **72**

Westminster and St. James's

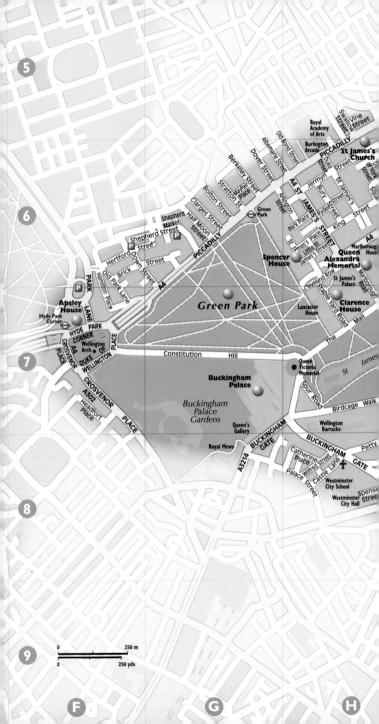

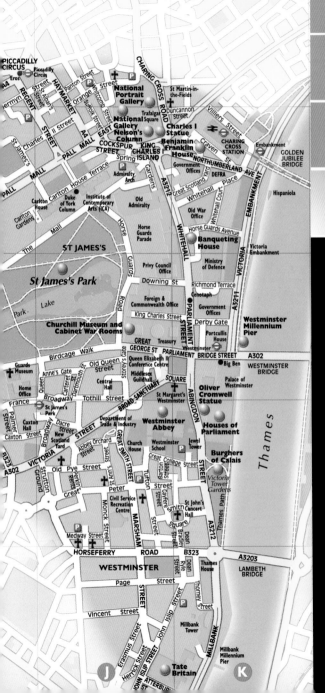

PICCADILLY CIRCUS
Piccadilly Circus
Eros

Panton Street
Orange Street

CHARING CROSS ROAD

St Martin-in-the-Fields

National Portrait Gallery

Duncannon Street

Trafalgar Square

National Gallery
Nelson's Column

Charles I Statue
Benjamin Franklin House

Craven Street

Villiers Street

CHARING CROSS STATION

Embankment

GOLDEN JUBILEE BRIDGE

COCKSPUR STREET
KING CHARLES ISLAND

NORTHUMBERLAND AVE

Spring Gardens

Government Offices

DEFRA

Great Scotland Yard

Whitehall Court

Admiralty Arch

Carlton House
Carlton House Terrace

Place

Hispaniola

Duke of York Column
Institute of Contemporary Arts (ICA)

Old Admiralty

Whitehall Place

Government Offices

VICTORIA EMBANKMENT

Carlton Gardens

Old War Office

PALL MALL

St James's

The Mall

Horse Guards Parade

Horse Guards Avenue

Banqueting House

ST JAMES'S

Guards Road

St James's Park

Lake

Privy Council Office

Victoria Embankment

Park

Ministry of Defence

Downing St

Richmond Terrace

Foreign & Commonwealth Office

Cenotaph

Government Offices

Churchill Museum and Cabinet War Rooms

King Charles Street

Derby Gate

Portcullis House

Westminster

Westminster Millennium Pier

Birdcage Walk

Treasury

GREAT GEORGE ST

PARLIAMENT

BRIDGE STREET

A302

Guards Museum

Old Queen Street

Queen Elizabeth II Conference Centre

WESTMINSTER BRIDGE

Anne's Gate

Storey's Gate

Big Ben

Palace of Westminster

Home Office

Carteret St

Dartmouth St

Central Hall

SQUARE

France

Caxton Hall

Broadway

Tothill Street

St Margaret's Westminster

Oliver Cromwell Statue

ABINGDON

Houses of Parliament

Palmer Street

St James's Park

Dacre Street

Departments of Trade & Industry

GREAT SMITH STREET

Westminster Abbey

Thames

VICTORIA STREET

Caxton Street

New Scotland Yard

Abbey Orchard Street

Church House

Westminster School

Jewel Tower

Burghers of Calais

Old Pye Street

Tufton Street

Great College Street

Abingdon Street

Victoria Tower Gardens

Peter Street

Civil Service Recreation Centre

MARSHAM

Smith Square

St John's Concert Hall

Medway Street

Monck Street

Dean Bradley Street

Dean Ryle Street

HORSEFERRY ROAD

B323

Thames House

A3203

LAMBETH BRIDGE

WESTMINSTER

Page Street

Millbank Tower

Vincent Street

John Islip Street

Thorney Street

MILLBANK

Millbank Millennium Pier

Erasmus Street

Herrick Street

JOHN ISLIP STREET

ATTERBURY

Tate Britain

J

K

Buckingham Palace

 TOP 25

HIGHLIGHTS

- The Queen's Gallery
- Changing of the Guard
- State Coach, Royal Mews
- Nash's façade, Quadrangle
- Gobelin tapestries in the Guard Room
- Throne Room
- Van Dyck's portrait of Charles I and family

TIPS

- To avoid the lines book a timed ticket in advance.
- Visit the quality royal souvenir shops.

Of the London houses now open to visitors, the Queen's own home is perhaps the most fascinating: Where else can you see a living sovereign's private art, drawing rooms and horse harnesses?

Yet another palace The British sovereigns have moved around London quite a bit over the years; from Westminster to Whitehall to Kensington and St. James's, and finally to Buckingham Palace. It was George III who in 1762 bought the prime-site mansion, Buckingham House, as a gift for his new bride, the 17-year-old Queen Charlotte, leaving St. James's Palace to be the official royal residence.

Grand improvements When the Prince Regent finally became King George IV in 1820, he and his architect, John Nash, made extravagant changes

Guards taking part in the traditional pageantry outside Buckingham Palace (far left). Buckingham Palace in all its glory (right). Crowds gather to watch a marching band on parade outside the palace gates (below left and right). Detail on the palace gates (below middle)

using Bath stone, all to be covered up by Edward Blore's façade added for Queen Victoria. Today, the 600 rooms and 16ha (40 acre) garden include the State Apartments, offices for the Royal Household, a cinema, swimming pool and the Queen's private rooms.

Open house The Queen inherited the world's finest private art collection. The Queen's Gallery, beautifully restyled by John Simpson, and opened for her Golden Jubilee in 2002, exhibits some of her riches. In the Royal Mews, John Nash's stables house gleaming fairy-tale coaches, harnesses and other apparel used for royal ceremonies. Don't miss the Buckingham Palace Summer Opening, when visitors can wander through the grand State Rooms, resplendent with gold, pictures, porcelain, tapestries and thrones.

THE BASICS

www.royal.gov.uk

➕ G7

✉ Buckingham Gate, SW1

☎ 020 7766 7300; Queen's Gallery 020 7766 7301; Royal Mews 020 7766 7302

🕐 Queen's Gallery daily 10–5.30, last admission 4.30. Royal Mews mid-Mar to end Oct Sat –Thu 11–4 (Aug–end Sep daily 10–5); last admission 45 min before closing. Closed Ascot week and ceremonial occasions. State Rooms, Buckingham Palace Aug–end Sep daily 9.45–6 (timed ticket every 15 min)

🚇 Victoria, Hyde Park Corner 🚃 Victoria

♿ Excellent 💷 Expensive

❓ No photography

Banqueting House

The Apothesis of James I *by Rubens*

THE BASICS

www.hrp.org.uk

✛ K6

✉ Whitehall, SW1

☎ 0844 482 7777

🕐 Mon–Sat 10–5; last admission 4.30. Closed 24 Dec–1 Jan, public hols and for functions

🚇 Westminster, Charing Cross, Embankment

♿ None

💷 Moderate

❓ Occasional lunchtime concerts

HIGHLIGHTS

● Sculpted head of Charles I
● Weathercock put on the roof by James II
● Rubens ceiling
● Allegory of James I between Peace and Plenty
● Allegory of the birth and coronation of Charles I
● Lunchtime concerts
● Whitehall river terrace in Embankment Gardens
● The video and self-guiding audio tour

It is chilling to imagine Charles I calmly crossing the park from St. James's Palace to be beheaded outside the glorious hall built by his father. The magnificent ceiling was painted for Charles by Flemish artist, Peter Paul Rubens.

Magnificent rooms This, all that remains of Whitehall Palace, was London's first building to be coated in smooth, white Portland stone. Designed by Inigo Jones and built between 1619 and 1622, it marked the beginning of James I's dream to replace the original sprawling Tudor palace with a 2,000-room Palladian masterpiece. In fact, it was only the banqueting hall that was built. Inside, the King hosted small parties in the crypt and presided over lavish court ceremonies upstairs.

Rubens ceiling The stunning ceiling was commissioned by James's son, Charles I. Painted between 1634 and 1636 by Peter Paul Rubens, the panels celebrate James I, who was also James VI of Scotland. Nine allegorical paintings show the unification of Scotland and England and the joyous benefits of wise rule.

The demise The palace has had a fair share of bad luck. Cardinal Thomas Wolsey lived so ostentatiously that he fell from Henry VIII's grace. Henry made it his and his successors' main London royal home. Charles I was beheaded here on 30 January 1649, and William III suffered from the dank river air. A fire in 1698 wiped out the Tudor building, leaving only the Banqueting House.

A first glance of the Houses of Parliament across the river is an impressive sight

Big Ben is for many the symbol of London: They love its tower, its huge clear clockface and its thundering hourly chimes. Summer tours of the whole building reveal its beauty, intriguing traditions and government workings.

Powerhouse for crown and state William the Conqueror made Westminster his seat of rule to watch over the London merchants. It was soon the heart of government for England, then Britain, then a globe-encircling empire. It was also the principal home of the monarchs until Henry VIII moved to Whitehall. Here the foundations of Parliament were laid according to Edward I's Model Parliament of 1295; a combination of elected citizens, lords and clergy. This developed into the House of Commons (elected Members of Parliament) and the House of Lords (unelected senior members of State and Church). Henry VIII's Reformation Parliament of 1529–36 ended Church domination of Parliament and made the Commons more powerful than the Lords.

Fit for an empire Having survived the Catholic conspiracy to blow up Parliament on 5 November 1605, most of the buildings were destroyed by a fire in 1834. Kingdom and empire needed a new headquarters. With Charles Barry's plans and A. W. Pugin's detailed design, a masterpiece of Victorian Gothic was created. Behind the façade, the Lords is on the left and the Commons on the right. If Parliament is in session, there is a flag on Victoria Tower or, at night, a light on Big Ben.

THE BASICS

www.parliament.uk

+ K8

✉ Westminster, SW1

☎ 020 7219 3000; Commons 020 7219 4272; Lords 020 7219 3107; tours 0870 906 3773; Jewel Tower 020 7222 2219

🕐 Visits to House of Commons when house is sitting Mon–Tue 2.30–10.30, Wed 11.30–7.30, Thu 10.30–6.30, Fri 9.30–3. Tours during summer recesses (Jul–end Oct); charge moderate. Non-UK residents can apply for tickets from their embassy or consulate. Jewel Tower Apr–end Oct daily 10–5; Nov–end Mar daily 10–4

🚇 Westminster

🚉 Waterloo

♿ Parliament free; tours expensive. Jewel Tower moderate

❓ State Opening of Parliament mid-Nov

HIGHLIGHTS

● View from Westminster Bridge
● Big Ben
● Summer tours
● St. Stephen's Hall
● Westminster Hall
● State Opening of Parliament
● Jewel Tower

National Gallery

TOP 25

Cooling off in Trafalgar Square (left), opposite the National Gallery (right)

THE BASICS

www.nationalgallery.org.uk

➕ J6

✉ Trafalgar Square, WC2

☎ 020 7747 2885

🕐 Mon, Tue, Thu–Sun 10–6, Wed 10–9. Closed Good Fri

🍴 Brasserie, café

Ⓒ Charing Cross, Leicester Square

🚆 Charing Cross

♿ Excellent 🎫 Free

❓ Guided tours (free daily 11.30 and 3.30, also Wed 6.30), lectures, films, audio guide, computer stations

HIGHLIGHTS

- *Virgin Enthroned*, Cenni di Peppi Cimabue
- Cartoon, Leonardo da Vinci
- *Pope Julius II*, Raphael
- *The Arnolfini Wedding*, van Eyck
- Equestrian portrait of Charles I by van Dyck
- *The Haywain*, John Constable
- *Madonna of the Pinks*, Raphael
- *The Archers*, Henry Raeburn
- *Sunflowers*, van Gogh
- *Mr and Mrs William Hallett*, Gainsborough
- *La Pointe de Hève*, Monet
- Restored entrance lobby and galleries

Here is a collection of tip-top pictures— and for free, so you can drop in for a few minutes' peace in front of Leonardo da Vinci's cartoon in the Sainsbury Wing or Rubens's ravishing *Samson and Delilah*.

Quality collection Founded in 1824 with just 38 pictures, the National Gallery now has about 2,000 paintings, all on show. Spread throughout William Wilkins's neoclassical building and the Sainsbury Wing extension, they provide an extremely high-quality, concise panorama of European painting from Giotto to Cézanne.

Free from the start Unusual for a national painting collection, the nucleus is not royal but the collection of John Julius Angerstein, a self-made financier. From the start it was open to all, free of charge, and provided a wide spectrum of British painting within a European context—aims that are still maintained. However, there is a charge for the temporary exhibitions in the Sainsbury Wing.

A first visit To take advantage of the rich artistic panorama, choose a room from each of the four chronologically arranged sections. Early paintings by Duccio di Buoninsegna, Jan van Eyck, Piero della Francesca and others fill the Sainsbury Wing. The West Wing has 16th-century pictures, including Michelangelo's *Entombment*, while the North Wing is devoted to 17th-century artists such as van Dyck, Rubens, Rembrandt and painters of the Dutch school. Tthe East Wing runs from Chardin through Gainsborough to Matisse and Picasso.

When you're done viewing art (left), the restaurant (right) is a welcome respite

National Portrait Gallery

It's fascinating to see what someone famous looks like and how they chose to be painted—for instance, you would never expect Francis Drake to be in red courtier's, rather than nautical clothes.

British record Founded in 1856 to collect portraits of the great and good in British life, and so inspire others to greatness, this now huge collection is the world's most comprehensive of its kind. There are oil paintings, watercolours, caricatures, silhouettes and photographs.

Start at the top The galleries, incorporating the Ondaatje Wing, are arranged in chronological order, starting on the top floor—reached by stairs or elevator. Tudor monarchs kick off a visual Who's Who of British history that moves through inventors, merchants, engineers, explorers and empire builders to modern politicians. Here you'll find Isambard K. Brunel, Robert Clive and Warren Hastings of India, Winston Churchill and Margaret Thatcher. There is Chaucer in his floppy hat, Kipling at his desk and A. A. Milne with Christopher Robin and Winnie-the-Pooh on his knee. Lesser-known sitters also merit a close look, such as the 18th-century portrait of the extensive Sharp Family, who formed an orchestra and played at Fulham every Sunday.

Modern times At first, the Victorians insisted on entry only after death, but this rule has been revised. Among the many contemporary portraits, you may find those of the football star David Beckham, and ex-Beatle Sir Paul McCartney.

THE BASICS

www.npg.org.uk
 J5
St. Martin's Place, WC2
020 7306 0055
Daily 10–6 (also Thu–Fri until 9pm); closed Good Fri
Café, rooftop restaurant
Leicester Square, Charing Cross
Charing Cross
Good
Free except for special exhibitions
Lectures, events

HIGHLIGHTS

● *Self-portrait with Barbara Hepworth*, Ben Nicholson
● Icon-like Richard II
● The Tudor Galleries
● *Samuel Pepys*, John Hayl
● *Queen Victoria*, Sir George Hayter
● *The Brontë Sisters*, Branwell Brontë
● *Isambard Kingdom Brunel*, John Callcott
● *Sir Peter Hall*, Tom Phillips
● Using the self-guiding audio tour
● An unfinished sketch of Jane Austen (c1810) by her sister, Cassandra

St. James's Park

St. James's Park is a great place to relax and has some lovely riverside spots

THE BASICS

✚ J7
✉ The Mall, SW1
☎ 020 7930 1793
🕐 Daily dawn to midnight
🍴 Inn the Park (▷ 80)
🚇 St. James's Park, Green Park, or Westminster
🚂 Victoria
♿ Very good 🎫 Free
❓ Changing the Guard (contact tourist information). Bird talks; guided walks

HIGHLIGHTS

● Springtime daffodils
● Whitehall views from the lake bridge
● Feeding the pelicans, 3pm
● Views to Buckingham Palace
● Duck Island in springtime

TIPS

● Inn the Park café opens early and closes late.
● The perfect setting for summer picnics.
● Consult the website beforehand.

Drop in to St. James's Park to eat a sandwich and laze on a deck chair while listening to the band's music; try spotting palaces across the duck-filled lake and over the tips of the weeping willows.

Royal heart St. James's Park is the oldest and most royal of London's nine royal parks, surrounded by the Palace of Westminster, St. James's Palace, Buckingham Palace and the remains of Whitehall Palace. Kings and their courtiers have been frolicking here since Henry VIII laid out a deer park in 1532 and built a hunting lodge that became St. James's Palace. James I began the menagerie, including pelicans, crocodiles and an elephant who drank a gallon of wine daily.

French order Charles II, influenced by Versailles, near Paris, redesigned the park to include a canal, Birdcage Walk (where he kept aviaries) and the gravelled Mall, where he played pell mell, a courtly French game similar to croquet. George IV, helped by John Nash and influenced by Humphrey Repton, softened the garden's formal French lines into the English style, making this 37ha (93-acre) park of blossoming shrubs and undulating, curving paths popular with romantics.

Nature As the park is an important migration point and breeding area for birds, two full-time ornithologists look after up to 1,000 birds from more than 45 species. Seek out the pelicans living on Duck Island, a tradition begun when the Russian Ambassador gave some to Charles II.

*Statues and columns
adorn the front
entrance to Tate
Britain*

Tate Britain

Moving through the galleries past Gainsborough portraits, Turner landscapes and Hepworth sculptures, this is an intimate social history of Britain told by its painters.

Two for one The Tate Gallery was opened in 1897, named after the sugar millionaire Henry Tate, who paid for the core building and donated his Victorian pictures to put inside it. Until 2000, the national collections of British and international modern art were housed there. Then, the international modern collection went to Bankside Power Station and was renamed Tate Modern (▷ 26). The national collection fills Henry Tate's refurbished building, which is now called Tate Britain.

British art The galleries are helpfully divided into four chronological suites. You can follow the visual story of British art from 1500 until today. Although paintings, sculptures, installations and works in other media will be changed regularly, you may well see van Dyck's lavish court portraits and richly coloured Pre-Raphaelite canvases. Do not miss the great Turner collection housed in the adjoining Clore Gallery.

Turner Prize Britain's most prestigious and controversial prize to celebrate young British talent is run by the Tate and awarded each autumn following an exhibition of nominees' works. Founded in 1984, winners have included Damien Hurst and Chris Ofili, while Tracey Emin, Sam Taylor-Wood and Tony Cragg have all been nominated.

THE BASICS

www.tate.org.uk

✚ J9

✉ Millbank, SW1, entrances on Millbank and Atterbury Street

☎ 020 7887 8000

🕐 Daily 10–5.50

🍴 Restaurant, café

Ⓜ Pimlico, Vauxhall, Westminster

🚊 Victoria

♿ Very good

✋ Free except for special exhibitions

❓ Full education schedule; audio tours

HIGHLIGHTS

- The Clore Gallery
- Thomas Gainsborough portrait
- *Flatford Mill*, Constable
- A William Blake vision
- A William Hogarth caricature
- A Barbara Hepworth stone or wood sculpture
- A work on paper by David Hockney
- *The Opening of Waterloo Bridge*, Constable
- Temporary exhibitions
- The Tate to Tate ferry

Thames River Cruise

HIGHLIGHTS

- Lambeth Palace
- Houses of Parliament
- London Eye
- St. Paul's Cathedral
- Tower Bridge
- Tower of London
- Thames Barrier

TIPS

- Shop around for the best deals.
- Tate boat plies between the two Tate galleries.
- Take a jacket, London weather changes quickly.

A cruise along the Thames is a leisurely way to see the city. It gives a new perspective to London's development and history, which is inextricably linked with this long and majestic river.

Wonderful sights Many companies run river cruises and water-buses along sections of the river. A particularly good stretch is from Westminster Pier in an easterly direction, which takes in a host of sights. This marks the point where the river enters central London and becomes a working highway, until recently lined with shipping, docks and warehouses. At this point the Thames flows between Lambeth Palace and the Houses of Parliament (▷ 65) and past the London Eye (▷ 24) and the Southbank complex (▷ 31) making a northern loop past the Victoria Embankment and toward

The Thames Flood Barrier (left). There are many fascinating sights to see aboard a Thames river bus (below right): Albert Bridge (top) and Waterloo Bridge (below left), to name a few

the Millennium Bridge, linking St. Paul's Cathedral (▷ 37) and Tate Modern (▷ 26).

Great bridges Beyond Shakespeare's Globe (▷ 31) and Southwark Cathedral (▷ 28) the river reaches London Bridge, the modern crossing that replaced the 1831 version, itself replacing its arched medieval predecessor. The next crossing is Tower Bridge, designed to allow tall ships passage between the city and the sea. On the north bank is the Tower of London (▷ 38), William the Conqueror's fort placed strategically to protect the Port.

Modern versus maritime From here the river goes through an area once dominated by docks and now redeveloped as smart office and residential blocks. Seafaring is the theme as the Thames reaches Greenwich (▷ 96) and then the Thames Barrier.

THE BASICS

✚ K7
✉ Start point:
Westminster Pier
Ⓤ Westminster
🚢 Circular Cruise
Westminster
(020 7936 2033;
www.crownriver.com)
City Cruises
(020 7740 0400;
www.citycruises.com)
Thames River Services
(020 7930 4097; www.
westminsterpier.co.uk)
Westminster Passenger
Service Association
(020 7930 2062;
www.wpsa.co.uk)

Westminster Abbey

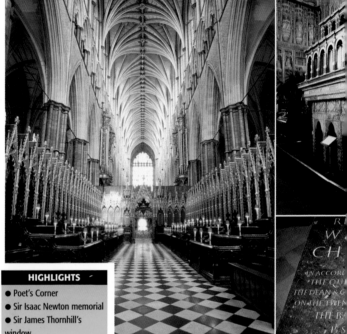

HIGHLIGHTS

- Poet's Corner
- Sir Isaac Newton memorial
- Sir James Thornhill's window
- Henry VII's Chapel
- Edward the Confessor's Chapel
- St. Faith's Chapel
- Tomb of the Unknown Warrior
- Little Cloister and College Garden
- Weekday sung evensong at 5pm

TIP

- Attend a service and hear the choirboys, accompanied by the abbey organ, which composer Henry Purcell (1659–95) once played.

The best time to be in the abbey is for the 8am service, sometimes held in tiny St. Faith's Chapel. Follow this with a wander in the silent nave and cloisters before the crowds arrive.

The kernel of London's second city It was Edward the Confessor who in the 11th century began the rebuilding of the modest Benedictine abbey church of St. Peter, which was consecrated in 1065. The first sovereign to be crowned there was William the Conqueror, on Christmas Day 1066. Successive kings were patrons, as were the pilgrims who flocked to the Confessor's shrine. Henry III (1216–72) employed Master Henry de Reyns to begin the Gothic abbey that stands today, and Henry VII (1485–1509) built his Tudor chapel with its delicate fan vaulting. Since William I, all

The choir stalls leading to the ornate gilt altar of Westminster Abbey (far left). The grand tomb of Edward the Confessor (top left). A memorial to Winston Churchill inside the Abbey (below left). A dizzying view up into the roof space of Westminster Abbey (right)

sovereigns have been crowned here—even after Henry VIII broke with Rome in 1533 and made himself head of the Church of England; and all were buried here up to George II (after which Windsor became the royal burial place ▷ 102).

Daunting riches The abbey is massive, full of monuments and very popular. From the nave's west end enjoy the view and Master Henry's achievement, then look over the Victorian Gothic choir screen into Henry V's chantry. Having explored the chapels, the royal necropolis and Poets' Corner, leave time for the quiet cloister with superb views of the flying buttresses supporting the nave. In the abbey museum you can see macabre wax effigies, including those of Queen Elizabeth I, Charles II and Lord Nelson, made using their death masks and real clothes.

THE BASICS

www.westminster-abbey.
org
✚ J8
✉ Broad Sanctuary, SW1;
entry by North Door
☎ 020 7222 5152
🕐 Abbey Mon–Sat times
vary; call or check website;
no photography. Abbey
Museum, College Garden
daily various hours. Closed
before special services,
Sun, 24–25 Dec, Good Fri
and Commonwealth Day
🍴 Café in cloisters
Ⓜ Westminster, St.
James's Park
🚌 Victoria
♿ Good
❓ Guided tours,
audio guides

More to See

APSLEY HOUSE (WELLINGTON MUSEUM)
www.english-heritage.org.uk
Splendid mansion built for Arthur Wellesley, Duke of Wellington (1759–1852). The sumptuous interior houses his magnificent collection of paintings and decorative arts.
➕ F7 ✉ Hyde Park Corner, W1 ☎ 020 7499 5676 🕐 Apr–end Oct Tue–Sun 10–5; Nov–end Mar 10–4 🚇 Hyde Park Corner 💷 Moderate

BENJAMIN FRANKLIN HOUSE
www.benjaminfranklinhouse.org
The Founding Father of the United States lived at this address for 15 years in the 18th century. Benjamin Franklin's historic house opened in 2006.
➕ K6 ✉ 36 Craven Street, WC2N ☎ 020 7839 2006 🕐 Wed–Sun 12–5 🚇 Charing Cross 💷 Moderate

BURGHERS OF CALAIS
Auguste Rodin's sculpture of muscular bronze citizens (1915).
➕ K8 ✉ Victoria Tower Gardens, SW1 🚇 Westminster

CABINET WAR ROOMS
www.iwm.org.uk
Two parts make up this museum: the evocative Cabinet War Rooms kept as they were during World War II, and the Churchill Museum opened in 2005.
➕ J7 ✉ Clive Steps, King Charles Street, SW1 ☎ 020 7930 6961 🕐 Daily 9.30–6 🚇 St. James's Park, Westminster 💷 Moderate

CHARLES I STATUE
This superb equestrian statue of Charles I was made by Hubert Le Sueur in 1633.
➕ J6 ✉ South side of Trafalgar Square 🚇 Charing Cross 🚉 Charing Cross

CLARENCE HOUSE
www.royal.gov.uk
Built for Prince William, Duke of Clarence and later William IV, this was the Queen Mother's London home, now renovated by its current resident, The Prince of Wales. All tickets are timed and must be prebooked.
➕ H7 ✉ Off the Mall, SW1 ☎ 020 7766 7303 🕐 Aug–end Sep daily 10–5.30 🚇 St. James's Park, Green Park 💷 Moderate

Red begonia flowers give a spectacular show in Green Park

The Burghers of Calais *in Parliament Square*

GREEN PARK

www.royalparks.gov.uk

Covering 16ha (40 acres), Green Park is famous for its mature trees, tree-lined avenues and spring daffodils. In the southwest is Wellington Arch.

🔲 G7 ✉ SW1 ☎ 020 7930 1793 ⏱ Daily dawn–dusk 🚇 Green Park, Hyde Park Corner 🎟 Free

NELSON'S COLUMN

Horatio, Viscount Nelson (1758–1805) went up on to his 52m (172ft) column in 1843; the hero died as he defeated the French and Spanish at Trafalgar. Sir Edwin Landseer sculpted the four guardian lions.

🔲 J6 ✉ Trafalgar Square 🚇 Charing Cross 🚉 Charing Cross

OLIVER CROMWELL STATUE

King-like Cromwell, Lord Protector of England from 1653 to 1658, looks across Parliament Square.

🔲 K8 ✉ Parliament Square 🚇 Westminster

QUEEN ALEXANDRA MEMORIAL

An art nouveau bronze designed by Alfred Gilbert, a memorial to Edward VII's Danish-born wife, commissioned by her daughter-in-law, Queen Mary.

🔲 H6 ✉ Marlborough Road, SW1 🚇 Green Park

ST. JAMES'S, PICCADILLY

www.st-james-piccadilly.org

Wren's chic church (1682–84) for local aristocracy has a sumptuous interior. Superb concerts.

🔲 H6 ✉ 197 Piccadilly, SW1 ☎ 020 7734 4511 ⏱ Daily 8–6.30 🍴 Café 🚇 Piccadilly Circus 🎟 Donation

SPENCER HOUSE

www.spencerhouse.co.uk

Lavishly restored Palladian mansion, a rare survivor of 18th-century aristo-cratic St. James's and Mayfair. Eight rooms with gilded decorations, period paintings and furniture. The restored garden opened in 2008.

🔲 H6 ✉ 27 St. James's Place, SW1 ☎ 020 7499 8620 ⏱ Sun 10.30–5.45, closed Jan and Aug. Booking advised, com-pulsory guided tour 🚇 Green Park 🎟 Expensive; no children under 10

Inside St. James's Church

Nelson's Column in Trafalgar Square

A Royal Tour

Take a stroll round St. James's, still evocative of times when aristocrats lived here and courtiers attended the sovereign.

DISTANCE: 3.2km (2 miles) **ALLOW:** 2 hours

START

ST. JAMES'S PARK (▷ 68)
St. James's Park

END

HYDE PARK CORNER (▷ 89)
Hyde Park Corner

❶ At the entrance to St. James's Park continue straight ahead to reach the lake. Cross the bridge and turn immediately right. At the fork go left.

❷ Glance right to see Big Ben (▷ 65). Walk on to the far northeast corner of the park and exit onto the Mall. Cross the Mall to the Institute of Contemporary Arts (▷ 79).

❸ Go around to the left of the ICA and up the steps to Waterloo Place. Turn left onto Pall Mall then right (a small road) into St. James's Square.

❹ Walk counterclockwise round the square. Look for the former home of Nancy Astor, the second woman to be elected to Parliament and the first to take her seat.

❽ Bear right and walk along the south edge of Green Park (▷ 75) to Hyde Park Corner and its statuary.

❼ Continue right along the side of St. James's Palace and right into Marlborough Road, past Queen's Chapel and Queen Alexandra Memorial (▷ 75). Rejoin the Mall at the bottom, turning right. Pass Clarence House garden and continue to Buckingham Palace (▷ 62).

❻ At the end of the street, cross St. James's Street and turn left toward St. James's Palace (▷ 68). Take the first right into Little St. James's Street and follow the road to Bridgewater House. In front is the entrance to Clarence House (▷ 74).

❺ Go past the East India Club and right into King Street. Look to the right to see Christie's (▷ 77) auction house.

WALK

WESTMINSTER AND ST. JAMES'S

Shopping

AGNEWS

This internationally renowned art gallery has been going since 1817. Specializes in European old masters from the 13th to the mid-19th centuries; British art from the 17th to the 20th centuries, in particular the Victorian era.
⊞ H6 ✉ 43 Old Bond Street, W1 ☎ 020 7290 9250 Ⓤ Green Park

BERRY BROS & RUDD

Opened as a grocer in 1699; the wines range from popular varieties to specialty madeiras, ports and clarets. Their own-label bottles are also good value. The service is perfect.
⊞ H6 ✉ 3 St. James's Street, SW1 ☎ 020 7396 9600 Ⓤ Green Park

CHRISTIE'S

Just viewing a sale at Christie's great rooms is an experience—and it costs nothing. Secondary salesrooms in South Kensington.
⊞ H6 ✉ 8 King Street, SW1 ☎ 020 7839 9060 Ⓤ Green Park

FORTNUM & MASON

Before going in, do not miss the clock, which has Messrs. Fortnum and Mason mincing forward each hour. Prices are high, but the shop-brand Fortnum's goods make perfect presents.
⊞ H6 ✉ 181 Piccadilly, W1 ☎ 020 7734 8040

Ⓤ Piccadilly Circus, Green Park

HATCHARDS

Opened in 1797; past patrons have included British army commander, the Duke of Wellington (1769–1852) and four-time prime minister William Gladstone (1809–98). Today's well-informed staff still know how to make book-buying a delicious and rewarding experience.
⊞ H6 ✉ 187 Piccadilly, W1 ☎ 020 7439 9921 Ⓤ Piccadilly Circus, Green Park

MAGGS BROTHERS

Make your appointment, then step into this Mayfair mansion to find an out-of-print book, a first edition or rare antiquarian book. Open Mon–Fri only.
⊞ G5 ✉ 50 Berkeley Square, W1 ☎ 020 7493 7160 Ⓤ Green Park

THOMAS GOODE LTD

Collectors of Meissen and Dresden need look no

PRIVATE GALLERIES

An indispensible tool for visitors getting to grips with commercial art galleries in London is the monthly *Galleries* magazine, available free from most galleries. With its maps and specialist subject index, information can be called up by area as well as subject.

further than this splendid showroom. Famous English names include Wedgwood, Minton, Spode & Royal Worcester.
⊞ F5 ✉ 19 South Audley Street, W1 ☎ 020 7499 2823 Ⓤ Green Park, Bond Street

TURNBULL & ASSER

If you want tradition and classic British design, then this is the shop for men who follow royalty when buying a shirt. Made to measure or off the peg, pricey but superb quality and service.
⊞ H6 ✉ 71–72 Jermyn Street, SW1 ☎ 020 7808 3000 Ⓤ Green Park, Piccadilly Circus

WATERFORD WEDGWOOD

The largest selection of handmade, full lead crystal Waterford glass—all made in Ireland—and Wedgwood china. Will phone the factory for special orders, help customers search for designs no longer made, and ship goods worldwide.
⊞ H6 ✉ 173–74 Piccadilly, W1 ☎ 020 7629 2614 Ⓤ Piccadilly Circus

WATERSTONE'S

Europe's spacious and largest bookshop stocks more than 250,000 titles and has a restaurant, café, internet area and staff who really know their subject.
⊞ H6 ✉ 203–206 Piccadilly, W1 ☎ 020 7851 2400 Ⓤ Piccadilly Circus

Entertainment and Nightlife

CADOGAN HALL
www.cadoganhall.com
London's major Christian Scientist church from 1904 to 1986 is now a fine concert hall just off Sloane Square, home to the Royal Philharmonic Orchestra and visited by a wide range of musicians and vocalists.

⊞ E9 ✉ 5 Sloane Square, SW1 ☎ 020 7730 4500
Ⓟ Sloane Square

COMEDY STORE
www.thecomedystore.co.uk
The best in stand-up comedy features impro-vised sketches from the Comedy Store Players. Big British TV and radio names who cut their teeth here include Rik Mayall, Ben Elton, Julian Clary and Steve Coogan.

⊞ J5 ✉ 1a Oxendon Street, SW1 ☎ 0870 060 2340
Ⓟ Piccadilly Circus, Leicester Square

DOVER STREET
www.doverstreet.co.uk
Large, popular basement, bedecked with candles, where the music can be jump jive, jazz, rhythm and blues or Big Band. The food is good.

⊞ G6 ✉ 8–9 Dover Street, W1 ☎ 020 7629 9813
Ⓟ Piccadilly Circus

INSTITUTE OF CONTEMPORARY ARTS (ICA)
www.ica.org.uk
Founded by Herbert Read, the ICA hosts cutting-edge art, screens seriously arty films and hosts performance artists who chart new territory in all media.

⊞ J6 ✉ The Mall, SW1 ☎ 020 7930 3647
Ⓟ Piccadilly Circus

ROYAL COURT THEATRE
www.royalcourttheatre.com
Here, London theatre was forever shaken up in the 1950s with John Osborne's *Look Back In Anger*, and today's playwrights follow in his wake.

⊞ E9 ✉ Sloane Square, SW1 ☎ 020 7565 5000
Ⓟ Sloane Square

ST. JAMES'S CHURCH PICCADILLY
www.st-james-piccadilly.org
Christopher Wren's sump-tuous setting for lunch-time and evening choral and orchestral concerts,

TICKET TIPS
Use the 'tkts' half-price ticket booth (in Leicester Square). Preview tickets and matinée tickets have reduced prices. Get up early and line up for one-day bargain tickets at the RNT and RSC. Go with friends and make a party booking at a reduced rate. Ask the National Theatre, Royal Court and other the-atres about special discounts on particular performances; and keep student and senior citizen cards ready. Remember, the show is the same wherever you sit!

plus star lecturers.

⊞ H6 ✉ 197 Piccadilly, W1 ☎ 020 7381 0441
Ⓟ Piccadilly Circus

ST. JOHN'S, SMITH SQUARE
www.sjss.org.uk
This handsome church is the setting for regular concerts, orchestral, chamber and solo, sometimes using its Klais organ. There's a good basement restaurant.

⊞ K8 ✉ Smith Square, SW1 ☎ 020 7222 1061
Ⓟ Westminster

ST. MARTIN-IN-THE-FIELDS
www.stmartin-in-the-fields.org
Baroque music is the focus here of the free lunchtime concerts (Monday, Tuesday and Friday) and candlelight evening concerts (Thursday, Friday and Saturday).

⊞ K5 ✉ Trafalgar Square, WC2 ☎ 020 7839 8362
Ⓟ Leicester Square

THE RITZ
www.theritzhotel.co.uk
To enter a bygone world, book up and dress up for dinner and a dance on a Friday or Saturday, held in London's most gracious and opulent dining room. Best to practice your two-step beforehand. For a more modest experience, go for afternoon tea or to the Rivoli Bar.

⊞ G6 ✉ 150 Piccadilly, W1 ☎ 020 7493 8181
Ⓟ Green Park

Restaurants

WESTMINSTER AND ST. JAMES'S · **RESTAURANTS**

PRICES

Prices are approximate, based on a 3-course meal for one person.

£££ over £60
££ £30–£60
£ under £30

GAUCHO (£££)

www.gauchorestaurants.co.uk
Carnivores will relish the steaks at this four-floor Argentinian restaurant. There are also tasty ceviches for a lighter meal. Excellent South American wines. The top floor has live music.
✚ H5 ✉ Swallow Street, W1 ☎ 020 7734 4040
🕐 Mon–Sat 12–12, Sun 12–11 Ⓟ Piccadilly Circus

GREENHOUSE (£££)

www.greenhouserestaurant.co.uk
Imaginative yet serious food by Antonin Bonnet who first made his name in France. Choose from the à la carte menu, the seasonal menu and a tasting menu. Superb wines.
✚ G6 ✉ 27a Hay's Mews, W1 ☎ 020 7499 3331
🕐 Mon–Fri 12–2.30, 6.45–11, Sat 6.45–11
Ⓟ Green Park

INN THE PARK (£)

www.innthepark.co.uk
Stylish British food with especially good cheeses. Michael Hopkins designed the wooden restaurant overlooking this year-round beautiful royal park with sweeping lawns.
✚ J7 ✉ St. James's Park, SW1 ☎ 020 7451 9999
🕐 Breakfast, lunch, dinner
Ⓟ St. James's Park

THE PORTRAIT RESTAURANT (££)

www.searcys.co.uk
In this museum restaurant every table benefits from the fine view. Reservations here are essential.
✚ J5 ✉ National Portrait Gallery, St. Martin's Place, WC2 ☎ 020 7312 2490
🕐 Sat–Wed 10–5, Thu, Fri 10am–10.30pm Ⓟ Leicester Square

INDIAN FOOD

London's 2,000 or so Indian restaurants cater to a well-informed local clientele. An Indian meal should have many dishes so, if you are a group, consider making a collective order and sharing. Tandoori dishes (cooked in a clay oven) make good starters. A North Indian meal's main course might include one or two meat offerings, two or three vegetable dishes, rice, a lentil or other pulse (such as chickpeas), and a variety of breads such as chapatti or naan–which are eaten hot, so order more as you go along. Remember the yogurt and pickles, and drink lassi (sweet or salty variations on buttermilk/yogurt) or beer.

TAMARIND (££)

www.tamarindrestaurant.com
Focusing on Mughal cuisine, Alfred Prassad has won the UK's first Michelin star for an Indian restaurant. Success has spawned a second restaurant from this management, Imli in Soho's Wardour Street.
✚ G6 ✉ 20 Queen Street, W1 ☎ 020 7629 3561
🕐 Mon–Fri 12–2.45, 6–11.30, Sat 6–11.30, Sun 12–2.45, 6.30–10.30 Ⓟ Green Park

VINCENT ROOMS (£)

Culinary students test their skills in cooking at the Vincent Rooms, which are usually pretty good even at this stage.
✚ H9 ✉ Westminster Kingsway College, Vincent Square, SW1 ☎ 020 7802 8391 🕐 Lunch Mon–Fri, phone for dinner times
Ⓟ Victoria, St. James's Park

THE WOLSELEY (££)

www.thewolseley.com
Jeremy King and Chris Corbin, who made the Ivy an institution, are repeating their success in a splendid former bank and car showroom; eat modern European dishes modestly or grandly. Start the day in art deco grandeur, or relax here after visiting the Royal Academy for a tasty tea.
✚ H6 ✉ 160 Piccadilly, W1 ☎ 020 7499 6996
🕐 Mon–Fri 7am–midnight, Sat 8am–midnight, Sun 8am–11pm Ⓟ Green Park, Piccadilly Circus

Soon after the British population flocked to Hyde Park to see the Great Exhibition in 1851, Chelsea, Knightsbridge and Belgravia developed into the upscale areas they are today, a delight to stroll through, with their stylish shops, bars and restaurants.

		Top 25	
Sights	84–89		
Shopping	90	Kensington Palace and Gardens ▷ 84	
Entertainment and Nightlife	91	Knightsbridge Shopping Spree ▷ 85	
		Natural History Museum ▷ 86	
Restaurants	92	Science Museum ▷ 87	
		Victoria and Albert Museum ▷ 88	

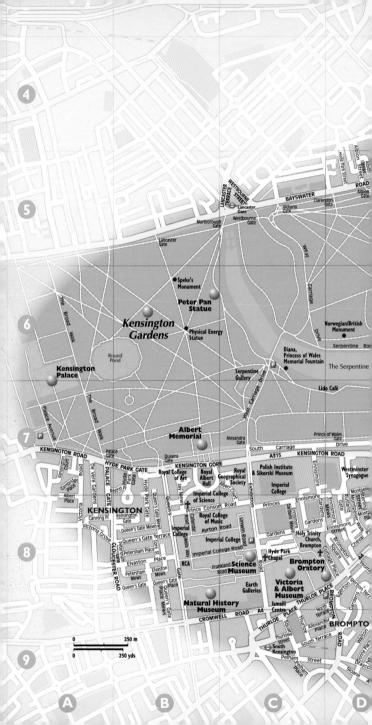

Kensington Palace and Gardens

Kensington Palace (right) and its gardens (middle). Albert Memorial (left)

THE BASICS

www.hrp.org.uk
⊞ A6
✉ Kensington Gardens, W8
☎ 0844 482 7777
Serpentine Gallery 020 7402 6075;
www.serpentinegallery.org
🕐 Mar–end Oct daily 10–6; Nov–end Feb 10–5; last entry 1 hour before closing. Serpentine Gallery daily 1–6
🍴 Café, Orangery (▷ 92)
🚇 High Street Kensington, Queensway
♿ Few
💷 Expensive; family tickets. Serpentine gallery free
❓ Guided tour every 30 min

HIGHLIGHTS

● King's Grand Staircase
● Presence Chamber
● Wind dial, King's Gallery
● King's Drawing Room
● Princess Victoria's dolls' house
● Round Pond
● Tea in the Orangery
● Italian Gardens

One of the reasons that King William III moved out of dank Whitehall Palace and into a mansion in tiny Kensington village was that he suffered from asthma and was looking for an area with cleaner air.

Perfect location The year he became king, 1689, William and his wife Mary bought their mansion, perfectly positioned for London socializing and country living. They brought in Sir Christopher Wren and Nicholas Hawksmoor to remodel and enlarge the house, and moved in for Christmas.

A special royal home Despite the small rooms, George I introduced palatial grandeur with Colen Campbell's staircase and state rooms. Meanwhile, Queen Anne added the Orangery (the architect was Nicholas Hawksmoor, the woodcarver Grinling Gibbons) and annexed a chunk of royal Hyde Park, a trick repeated by George II's wife, Queen Caroline, who created the Round Pond and Long Water to complete the 110ha (275-acre) Kensington Gardens. Today, a variety of trees are the backdrop for sculptures (George Frampton's fairytale *Peter Pan*), monuments, and contemporary exhibitions at the Serpentine Gallery.

Special childhood On 24 May 1819, Queen Victoria was born here. She spent her childhood in rooms overlooking the gardens (now filled with Victoria memorabilia) and, on 20 June 1837, learned here she was to be queen. There is a permanent exhibition of the Queen's and Princess Diana's clothes.

The Edwardian façade of Harrods (right) conceals a wonderful food hall (left)

Knightsbridge Shopping Spree

London's smartest and most expensive real estate conurbation, with shops and price tags to match. If you have a need for some exhilarating retail therapy, Knightsbridge is for you.

Stylish shops As you leave the Underground station (Sloane Street exit) you'll see Harvey Nichols (▷ 90), London's most fashionable department store. On emerging from Harvey Nichols, head back toward the Underground and continue along Brompton Road. Opposite is a huge Burberry store, known for its distinctive tan-and-grey check design. On the left as you walk toward the canopied shopfront of Harrods (▷ 90) is Swarovski with window displays of diamond jewellery. Leave Harrods by the Hans Road exit and you'll see lingerie store Rigby & Peller across the street.

Even more stylish shops Return to Brompton Road and pass Mulberry before turning left to reach Beauchamp Place on the left. On the right is the Map House, with precious maps and engravings. At the top of Beauchamp Place, turn right into Walton Street. Along both sides of Walton Street are shops selling a selection of jewellery. At the southern end turn left into Draycott Avenue and walk up this street to turn left round Joseph, which sells beautiful women's clothing. Soon you'll reach Sloane Avenue. On the right is the Conran Shop, an emporium filled with stylish household items, Paul Smith and Kenzo. Continue down Sloane Avenue for King's Road and the Sloane Square tube.

THE BASICS

➕ D7–8

✉ Knightsbridge

🍴 Harvey Nichols restaurants and café-bars on the 4th and 5th floors, and a sushi bar on the 5th floor. The Boxwood Café in the Berkeley Hotel (Wilton Place, 020 7235 1010, lunch, dinner daily) is a Gordon Ramsey restaurant

Ⓤ Knightsbridge

HIGHLIGHTS

● Food halls at Harrods
● Designer dresses at Harvey Nichols
● Boutiques on Walton Street

TIPS

● In Harrods, check out the day's events, shows and demos.
● If you need a special outfit, no staff are more helpful than at Harvey Nichols.
● If it rains, stay put in Harrods and visit the spa.

Natural History Museum

TOP 25

Exhibits at the Natural History Museum (left), including a diplodocus skeleton (right)

THE BASICS

www.nhm.ac.uk

✚ B8

✉ Cromwell Road, SW7; also entrance on Exhibition Road

☎ 020 7942 5000

🕐 Daily 10–5.50

🍴 Meals, snacks, picnic areas

Ⓢ South Kensington

♿ Excellent 🆓 Free

❓ Regular tours, lectures, films, workshops

HIGHLIGHTS

● Cromwell Road façade
● Giant gold nugget
● Fossilized frogs
● The Vault, a gallery of crystals, gems and meteorites
● Restless Surface Gallery
● Tank Room in the Darwin Centre

TIPS

● Use the side entrance on Exhibition Road.
● It's huge: plan your visit carefully.

Before you go in, look at the museum building. It looks like a Romanesque cathedral and is wittily decorated with a zoo of animals to match its contents: extant animals on the west side, extinct ones on the east side.

Two museums in one Overflowing the British Museum, the Life Galleries were moved to Alfred Waterhouse's honey-and-blue-stripe building in 1880. They tell the story of life on earth. The story of the earth itself is told in the Earth Galleries, beginning with a 300-million-year-old fossil of a fern. The Darwin Centre uses IT to make the most of the museum's 70 million objects and the work of its 300 or so scientists accessible worldwide. A second phase due to open in 2009 will provide a much-needed new home for the museum's botany and entomology departments.

The Life Galleries The nave of Waterhouse's cathedral contains a plaster cast of the vast skeleton of the 150-million-year-old diplodocus (the original is in the US). Lively exhibition galleries focus on the relevance of the dinosaur world, the human body, mammals, birds, the marine world today and 'creepy crawlies' (the 800,000 known species of insect are added to every year).

The Earth Galleries These offer a fascinating exploration of our planet, which includes the effects of natural forces on the earth such as earthquakes and the gemstones and minerals that lie beneath the earth's crust.

Hand-on-exhibits keep kids amused for hours (left) and there's lots for adults, too (right)

Science Museum

Even if you are no scientist, it's thrilling to understand how a plane flies, how Newton's reflecting telescope worked, or how we receive satellite television. You'll find answers using hands-on interactives. This is science made fun.

Industry and Science Opened in 1857, this museum comes closest to fulfilling Prince Albert's educational aims when he founded the South Kensington Museums after the Great Exhibition of 1851. Its full title is the National Museum of Science and Industry. Over the seven floors, which contain more than 60 collections, the story of human industry, discovery and invention is recounted through various tools and products, from exquisite Georgian cabinets to a satellite launcher.

Science made fun People of all ages get excited by what they see here. You can see how vital everyday objects were invented and then developed for use. The spinning wheel, steam engine, car and television have changed our lives. The industrial society in which we live could not do without plastic, but how is it made? The galleries vary from rooms of beautiful 18th-century objects to in-depth explanations of abstract concepts: You can use the hands-on equipment in Flight Lab to learn the basic principles of flying. The Wellcome Museum of the History of Medicine, on the top floors, includes an exhibit on prehistoric bone surgery. The interactive Challenge of Materials and the high-tech Wellcome Wing explore science, technology and the complex world.

THE BASICS

www.sciencemuseum.org.uk

✚ C8

✉ Exhibition Road, SW7

☎ 0870 870 4868

🕐 Daily 10–6

🍴 Restaurants, cafés, picnic area in basement

Ⓢ South Kensington

♿ Excellent (☎ 020 7942 4446 helpline)

💷 Free; IMAX cinema expensive; Virtual Voyager moderate

❓ Guided tours, demonstrations, historic characters, lectures, films, workshops

HIGHLIGHTS

● Demonstrations
● Taking part in Launch Pad
● The hands-on basement area
● Puffing Billy
● 18th-century watches and clocks
● The Wellcome Wing
● Historical characters explaining their achievements

TIP

● Head for the higher, quieter floors to escape the crowds.

Victoria and Albert Museum

The Victoria and Albert Museum, known as the V&A, holds a huge collection of artworks

THE BASICS

www.vam.ac.uk

➕ C8

✉ Cromwell Road, SW7

☎ 020 7942 2000

🕐 Daily 10–5.45 (Fri 10–10)

🍴 Restaurant, café

Ⓜ South Kensington

♿ Very good

👆 Free

❓ Free daily guided, introductory tours. Talks, courses, demonstrations, workshops and concerts

HIGHLIGHTS

● British Galleries
● India and Islamic Galleries
● The Jewellery Gallery
● Glass Gallery
● The silver collection in restored rooms
● Canning Jewel
● Raphael Gallery
● Architecture Gallery
● The Hereford Screen

TIPS

● Hang out in the courtyard.
● Join a gallery tour or talk.
● Evening openings have a good atmosphere.

Part of the Victoria and Albert Museum's glory is that each room is unexpected; it may contain a French boudoir, plaster casts of classical sculptures or exquisite contemporary glass.

A vision The V&A, as it is fondly known, started as the South Kensington Museum. It was Prince Albert's vision: Arts and science objects available to all people to inspire them to invent and create, with the accent on commercial design and crafts-manship. Since it opened in 1857, its collection has become so encyclopedic and international, it's now the world's largest decorative arts museum.

Bigger and bigger Its size is unmanageable: 11km (7 miles) of gallery space on six floors. Its content is even more so: Barely 5 per cent of the 44,000 objects in the Indian department can be on show. Larger museum objects include whole London house façades, grand rooms and the Raphael Cartoons. Despite this, contemporary work has been energetically bought: More than 60 per cent of furniture entering the museum is 20th century.

Riches and rags Not every object in the V&A is precious: There are everyday things, unique pieces and opportunities to discover a fascination for a new subject—perhaps lace, ironwork, tiles or Japanese textiles. See the lavishly refurbished British Galleries, and the Whiteley Silver Galleries that show a magnificent collection of European silver and the Islamic Gallery opened in 2006.

ALBERT MEMORIAL

George Gilbert Scott's lavish memorial dedicated to the creator of South Kensington, Prince Albert.

➕ B7 ✉ Alexandra Gate, Kensington Gardens, SW7 🚇 South Kensington

BROMPTON ORATORY

www.bromptonoratory.com

Standing next door to the V&A, the flamboyant Oratory of St. Philip Neri was built in 1876 and given a sumptuous, sculpture-filled interior.

➕ C8 ✉ Brompton Road, SW7 ☎ 020 7808 0900 🕐 Daily 6.30am–8pm 🚇 South Kensington 💷 Donation

HOLY TRINITY, SLOANE SQUARE

www.holytrinitysloanesquare.co.uk

London's best Arts and Crafts church, built between 1888 and 1890 and designed by J. D. Sedding, has glass by Burne-Jones, William Morris and others. Note the huge east window with 48 panels depicting saints.

➕ E9 ✉ Sloane Square, SW1 ☎ 020 7730 7270 🕐 Mon–Sat 8.30–5.30, Sun 8.30–1.30 🚇 Sloane Square 💷 Donation

HYDE PARK

www.royalparks.gov.uk

One of London's largest open spaces, tamed by 18th-century royalty.

➕ E6 ✉ W2 ☎ 020 7298 2100 🕐 Daily 5am–midnight 🍴 Restaurant, café 🚇 Marble Arch, High Street Kensington, Hyde Park Corner 💷 Free

PETER PAN STATUE

George Frampton's statue (1912) commemorating J. M. Barrie's creation, the boy who never grew up stands in Kensingston Gardens.

➕ B6 ✉ Long Water, Kensington Gardens 🚇 Lancaster Gate

THE WALLACE COLLECTION

www.wallacecollection.org

The product of five generations of discerning art collectors of the Hertford family fills their London mansion. Good restaurant in the now roofed courtyard.

➕ F4 ✉ Hertford House, Manchester Square, W1 ☎ 020 7563 9500 🕐 Daily 10–5 🍴 Restaurant, café 🚇 Marble Arch, Bond Street 💷 Free

Exquisite stained glass inside Holy Trinity Church

Brompton Oratory

Shopping

GENERAL TRADING COMPANY

Chic, small-scale department store with quality buys in all areas from china to gardening. Good mail-order catalogue.
E9 ✉ 2 Symons Street, SW1 ☎ 020 7730 0411 Ⓢ Sloane Square

HARRODS

This vast emporium contains just about everything anyone could want. Apart from the revamped fashion departments, do not miss the spectacular food halls. Some 23 restaurants and bars provide refreshment.
D8 ✉ 87–135 Brompton Road, SW1 ☎ 020 7730 1234 Ⓢ Knightsbridge

HARVEY NICHOLS

London's classiest clothes shop, from its original storefront window displays to the well-stocked fashion floors. Chic, popular restaurant.
E7 ✉ 67 Brompton Road, SW1 ☎ 020 7235 5000 Ⓢ Knightsbridge

HAYNES HANSON & CLARK

This is a treat for the connoisseur, especially those keen on Burgundy. Much buying is direct from the wine estates.
F8 ✉ 25 Eccleston Street, SW1 ☎ 020 7259 0102 Ⓢ Knightsbridge

JEANETTE HAYHURST

One of the few places to find old glass, especially British pieces. Also stocks interesting studio glass.
Off map ✉ 32a Kensington Church Street, W8 ☎ 020 7938 1539 Ⓢ High Street Kensington

JIMMY CHOO

Guaranteed to sell the highest-heeled shoes in town. Set in the affluent Brompton Cross area it's worth taking a look and trying something on.
D9 ✉ 169 Draycott Avenue, SW3 ☎ 020 7584 6111 Ⓢ South Kensington

KENSINGTON CHURCH STREET

Specialist antiques shops run by knowledgeable dealers dot the length of this characterful street.
Off map ✉ Church Street, W8 Ⓢ High Street Kensington

LULU GUINNESS

Sleek modern shop

MAKE A PICNIC

With so many parks and benches in London, a picnic makes a good break from sightseeing or shopping. The big stores have seductive food halls and stock wine; see Harrods, Selfridges, Fortnum & Mason and Marks & Spencer. Old Compton Street is a food shopper's delight; see also Clarke's Bakery (✉ 122 Kensington Church Street, W8) and other cafés that sell their own prepared food to take out.

selling quirky 1950s handbags, hats and shoes. Bags in every shape, from spiders' webs to flower baskets. Celebrities shop here. Branch in the City's Royal Exchange.
E9 ✉ 3 Ellis Street, SW1 ☎ 020 7823 4828 Ⓢ Sloane Square

MARKS & SPENCER

Most people buy something at M&S. Clothes now have sharper styles, and the food departments offer an exceptional range of products.
E4 ✉ 458 Oxford Street, W1 ☎ 020 7935 7954 Ⓢ Marble Arch

PETER JONES

After a total renovation, this sister store to John Lewis, is back in the top league of London one-stop shopping experiences. Quality good design and sensible staff, plus advisory, packing and pampering services. Café and cocktail bar.
E9 ✉ Sloane Square, SW1 ☎ 020 7730 3434 Ⓢ Sloane Square

URBAN OUTFITTERS

Always changing; always supplying trend-conscious youngsters. Check out the latest and browse through the streetwear and newest accessories. Other branches.
Off map ✉ 36–38 Kensington High Street, W8 ☎ 020 7761 1001 Ⓢ High Street Kensington

Entertainment and Nightlife

BOISDALE
www.boisdale.co.uk
London's top malt whisky bar emphazises the Scottish theme with the odd tartan furnshings. Cozy dark bar and an attactive courtyard.
 F8 ✉ 15 Eccleston Street, SW1 ☎ 020 7730 6922 🚇 Victoria

BUSH HALL
www.bushhallmusic.co.uk
Formerly a ballroom and a snooker hall, reopened in 2000 as a small concert hall staging classical concerts, recitals, jazz and rock concerts.
✚ Off map ✉ 310 Uxbridge Road, Shepherd's Bush, W12 ☎ 020 8222 6955 🚇 Shepherd's Bush

CINÉ LUMIÈRE
www.institut-francais.org.uk
Part of the French government's hub of language and culture. Shows French films and other European and world cinema.
✚ B9 ✉ Institut Français, 17 Queensberry Place, SW7 ☎ 020 7073 1350 🚇 South Kensington, Gloucester Road

HOLLAND PARK THEATRE
www.operahollandpark.com
Confusingly, this is highly acclaimed opera, not theatre, which is staged beneath a canopy in one of London's most lush and romantic parks.
✚ Off map ✉ Holland Park, Kensington High Street, W8 ☎ 0845 230 9769 🚇 Holland Park

NOTTING HILL ARTS CLUB
www.nottinghillartsclub.com
Diversity and originality results from artists and DJs meeting here and gelling ideas.
✚ Off map ✉ 21 Notting Hill Gate, W11 ☎ 020 7460 4459 🚇 Notting Hill Gate

ROYAL ALBERT HALL
www.royalalberthall.com
Grand Victorian building holding 6,000 spectators; boxing, tennis and sumo-wrestling events fill the hall as successfully as the annual 'Prom' season, the Henry Wood Promenade Concerts. Running from mid-July to mid-September there are nightly concerts and always the cheap 'prom' tickets to stand or sit on the floor of the pit—no seats—among enthusiastic but impoverished music students.
✚ B7 ✉ Kensington Gore, SW7 ☎ 020 7589 8212 🚇 South Kensington

ROYAL COURT/ JERWOOD THEATRE UPSTAIRS
www.royalcourttheatre.com
Lofty artistic reputation; presents only new work by leading or emerging playwrights—a bookshop sells play texts. The main theatre seats 400, the studio 60.
✚ E9 ✉ Sloane Square, SW1 ☎ 020 7565 5000 🚇 Sloane Square

606 CLUB
www.606club.co.uk
West London's best small jazz club is open all week and books musicians with impeccable credentials. You may even catch gospel or blues performances. Note that alcohol is served only with food and the music cover charge is added to the cost of the meal.
✚ Off map ✉ Lots Road, SW10 ☎ 020 73953 🚇 Earls Court, Fulham Broadway

TRADER VICS
The South Seas meet Park Lane in this Tahitian-inspired bar in the Hilton Hotel. Pricey but fun, the tropical cocktails are a work of art. The bar is open daily.
✚ F6 ✉ 22 Park Lane, W1K ☎ 020 7208 4113 🚇 Hyde Park Corner

REVIVED THEATRES

Some old London theatres have been revived. Andrew Lloyd Webber restored his 1880s Cambridge Theatre. The Theatre Royal, Haymarket, has new gold leaf, while the Savoy and the Criterion have been meticulously restored. Out of the West End, the Richmond Theatre is a treat. On the South Bank, there is the splendidly ornate Old Vic Theatre and the small-scale Globe theatre opened in 1997, designed in the manner of Burbage's original where Shakespeare worked.

Restaurants

PRICES

Prices are approximate, based on a 3-course meal for one person.

£££	over £60
££	£30–£60
£	under £30

AMAYA (££)

www.realindianfood.com
The kebab is lifted to a fine food in this luxurious upscale Indian setting.
➕ E8 ✉ Halkin Arcade, SW1 ☎ 020 7823 1166 🕐 Mon–Sat 12.30–2.15, 6–11.15, Sun 12.45–2.45, 6–10.30 🚇 Knightsbridge

LE GAVROCHE (£££)

www.le-gavroche.co.uk
Albert's Roux's son sticks to classic French, but lighter; amazing wines, grand setting.
➕ E5 ✉ 43 Upper Brook Street, W1 ☎ 020 7408 0881 🕐 Mon–Fri 12–2, 6.30–11, Sat 6.30–11 🚇 Marble Arch

KENSINGTON PALACE ORANGERY (£)

www.digbytrout.co.uk
Elegant eating in an 18th-century royal building overlooking the palace's formal gardens. Perfect English setting for afternoon tea—cucumber sandwiches or scones with jam and cream.
➕ A6 ✉ Kensington Palace, Kensington Gardens, W8 ☎ 020 7376 0239 🕐 Mar–end Oct daily 10–6; Nov–end Mar daily 10–5 🚇 High Street Kensington

MAGGIE JONES'S (££)

A Kensington institution much-loved for its informality, wine list and no-nonsense British food.
➕ Off map ✉ 6 Old Court Place, Kensington Church Street, W8 ☎ 020 7937 6462 🕐 Daily 12.30–2.30, 6–11 (Sun 10.30) 🚇 High Street Kensington

MAZE (££)

www.gordonramsay.com
Jason Atherton's imaginative haute cuisine in a congenial atmosphere; a real pleasure.
➕ F5 ✉ Marriott Hotel, Grosvenor Square, W1 ☎ 020 7107 0000 🕐 Mon–Sat 12–2.30, 6–10.30 🚇 Bond Street

AMERICAN EXPERIENCE

America's fast food arrived long before its quality cuisine and restaurant style became established. Better burger bars include The Ultimate Burger and Gourmet Burger Kitchen chains. Upscale options include Joe Allen (▷ 57), Christopher's (▷ 57) and PJ's (✉ 52 Fulham Road, SW3 ☎ 020 7581 0025). Other good-value places to hang out are: Big Easy ✉ 332–334 King's Road, SW3 ☎ 020 7352 4071; Eagle Bar Diner ✉ 3–5 Rathbone Place, W1 ☎ 020 7637 1418; The Hard Rock Café ✉ 150 Old Park Lane, W1 ☎ 020 7514 1700.

NOBU (£££)

www.noburestaurants.com
New York's Nobuyuki Matsuhisa brings his pan-American Japanese cooking to London. Equally pricey outpost Ubon, at Canary Wharf.
➕ F7 ✉ Metropolitan Hotel, 19 Old Park Lane, W1 ☎ 020 7447 4747 🕐 Mon–Fri 12–2.15, 6–10.15, Sat 6–11.15, Sun 6–9.45 🚇 Hyde Park Corner

ROYAL CHINA (£)

www.royalchinagroup.co.uk
Reserve a table or join the justifiably long lines for the best dim sum in town. There are four branches.
➕ A5 ✉ 13 Queensway, W2 ☎ 020 7221 2535 🕐 Mon–Thu 12–11, Fri–Sat 12–11.30, Sun 11–10 🚇 Queensway

SALLOOS (££)

Consistently perfect Pakistani dishes from the North-Western Frontier; ideal for meat lovers.
➕ E8 ✉ 62–64 Kinnerton Street, SW1 ☎ 020 7235 4444 🕐 Mon–Sat 12–2.15, 7–11 🚇 Knightsbridge

TOM AIKENS (£££)

www.tomaikens.co.uk
Delicious haute cuisine and superb service to be enjoyed in a fresh, contemporary setting. Good value set-price menu and tasting menu available.
➕ D9 ✉ 43 Elystan Street, SW3 ☎ 020 7584 2003 🕐 Mon–Fri 12–2.30, 6.45–11 🚇 South Kensington

London has its many and diverse sights scattered for miles outside the heart of the city. While Regent's Park, Portobello Road and Hampstead are just a short tube ride away, others deserve a well-planned day trip.

Sights	96–102
Walk	103
Shopping	104
Entertainment and Nightlife	105
Restaurants	106

Top 25

Greenwich ▷ 96

Portobello Road Market ▷ 97

Royal Botanic Gardens, Kew ▷ 98

A10

Wood Green

A1055

M11

A113

Epping Forest

A406

REDBRIDGE

Tottenham

WALTHAM FOREST

A1400

A105

A503

HARINGEY

Walthamstow

A12

...sbury ...k

Walthamstow Marshes

A104

A107

Leytonstone

Wanstead Park

A406

Leyton

A117

Hackney Marshes

Wanstead Flats

A10

A12

Dalston

HACKNEY

Victoria Park

Stratford

East Ham

V&A Museum of Childhood

Mile End Park

A11

NEWHAM

A13

Holborn

Whitechapel Art Gallery

A12

A124

CITY

A1020

A100

Museum in Docklands

Firepower Museum

SOUTHWARK

Canary Wharf

Thames

Woolwich

Southwark Park

Burgess Park

GREENWICH

Woolwich Common

Peckham

New Cross

Greenwich Park

A207

A2

Black Heath

A205

Eltham Common

Oxleas Wood

Peckham Rye Park

LEWISHAM

A20

A2

Dulwich Picture Gallery

A205

Dulwich Park

Dulwich

A212

A20

Crystal Palace

Crystal Palace Park

Elmstead Woods

A208

A214

Beckenham Place Park

A21

Sundridge Park

A212

A215

A222

A232

Petts Wood

BROMLEY

Jubilee Country Park

A222

A232

A232

A232

CROYDON

A2022

A232

A212

0 ___ 4 km

0 ___ 2 miles

Greenwich

Detail of façade of the Old Royal Naval College (left). The Royal Observatory (right)

Detail of façade of the Old Royal Naval College (left). The Royal Observatory (right)

THE BASICS

➕ Off map at S7
✉ Greenwich, SE10
🍴 Restaurants and cafés
🚉 DLR Greenwich Cutty Sark
🚢 From Westminster

Old Royal Naval College and *Cutty Sark*
🕐 Grounds daily 8–6; Painted Hall and Chapel Mon–Sat 10–5
The Queen's House
🕐 Daily 10–4.30
The Royal Observatory and Planetarium
🕐 Daily 10–5
National Maritime Museum
🕐 Sep–Jul daily 10–5; Jul–Sep 10–6

HIGHLIGHTS

● *Captain Augustus Keppel* by Sir Joshua Renolds (Queen's House)
● Maritime equipment at the National Maritime Museum
● Winter star gazing at the Royal Observatory

This historic London district is a highly recommended day out, enthralling children and adults with science, sea stories and an excellent art collection. The town itself has a market, restaurants and a park.

Old Royal Naval College and the *Cutty Sark*
Your first stop should be at the *Cutty Sark*, once one of the fastest tea clippers but now a charred shell after a fire in 2007. It's being restored under a protective tent. Continue into the main quadrangle of the College. With your back to the Thames, the remarkable Painted Hall is on the right and was the sailor's dining room.

Art and maritime heritage At the foot of Greenwich Park, the Queen's House and National Maritime Museum stand adjacent to each other. The Queen's House is beautifully proportioned but the real surprise is the outstanding art collection inside. The National Maritime Museum is crammed with hands-on exhibits that answer pressing questions such as why the sea is salty. Boats on display range from small dinghies to the *Miss Britain III*, the first powerboat to top 100mph. Don't miss the fascinating collection of navigational equipment.

Astronomical delights Inside Sir Christopher Wren's cramped Observatory small galleries explain how time is measured. But the new astronomy galleries of the Planetarium next door merit much more time; they're modern, engaging and exciting but don't simplify the bigger questions about the universe.

Crowds flock to Portobello Road Market (left) for the specialist stalls (right)

Portobello Road Market

Spend a Saturday wandering down Portobello Road, peering at the stalls and dipping into the shops behind them to seek out a special piece of china, or a fascinating piece of glass.

Portobello Road Originally a lane leading down to Porto Bella Farm, this road has been a market site for a century. Gypsies traded horses and herbs here in the 1870s; but the antiques dealers only arrived in the late 1940s. Today it is one of Britain's longest street markets and is really a series of markets that spill into surrounding streets that sell almost everything imaginable. If you want a daylong party of fascination, fun and friendliness, come here on any Saturday.

More than just stalls Starting at the top, there are the established specialist antiques shops for maps, silver, medals, etc, where bargains are few. Don't miss Lipka arcade and the 20th Century theatre, opposite. Farther down, where the stalls begin, the stock is more varied and visitors join locals in the pubs and cafés to discuss values and possible acquisitions. Here you find antique clothes, records and china next to contemporary ceramics and jewellery. Explore the by-roads, too.

For something different After the vegetable and organic food stalls you go under the Westway fly-over, where there are restorative cafés. The tone changes. Here, look for funky bric-a-brac, as well as cutting-edge street fashion, vintage clothes and even second-hand bicycles.

THE BASICS

www.portobelloroad.co.uk
🞥 Off map at A5
✉ Market Office: 72 Tavistock Road, W11
🕐 Mon–Wed, Sat 8–7, Thu 8–1, Fri 8–6
🚇 Notting Hill Gate

HIGHLIGHTS

● Marringdean Antiques for Staffordshire china
● Spooky stuffed animals sold in Natural History
● The clocks and watches in Admiral Vernon arcade
● Henry Gregory's English games

TIPS

● Saturday is by far the best day, when the antiques dealers set up stalls in the street.
● No price is totally fixed; bargain hard.
● It is true that the early bird finds the best prices.
● Join locals buying a treat at Tom's Delicatessen on Westbourne Grove.

Royal Botanic Gardens, Kew

Set beside the Thames (right), the gardens feature several splendid greenhouses (left)

THE BASICS

www.kew.org
+ Off map at A9
✉ Kew Road, Kew
☎ 020 8332 5655
🕐 Daily from 9.30am; closing time varies
🍴 Restaurants, cafés
Ⓠ Kew Garden
Ⓡ Kew Bridge
▭ Kew pier
& Excellent 💷 Expensive
? Guided tours 11, 2 from Victoria Gate; orchid show Feb–end Mar

HIGHLIGHTS

● Arriving by riverboat
● Restored Kew Palace
● Gallery walks, Palm House
● Temperate House
● Springtime in the woods and dells
● Oak Avenue to Queen Charlotte's Cottage
● Evolution exhibition

TIP

● Take the Kew Explorer, a train that tours all the key sites in 40 minutes. Tickets are £2, available from the main entrance, from 11am.

Whether the trees are shrouded in winter mists, the azaleas are bursting with blossoms, or the lawns are dotted with summer picnickers, Kew Gardens never fail to work their magic.

Royal beginnings The 120ha (300-acre) gardens containing 44,000 different plants and many glorious greenhouses, make up the world's foremost botanical research centre. It began modestly: George III's mother, Princess Augusta, planted 4ha (9 acres) around tiny Kew Palace in 1759, helped by gardener William Aiton and botanist Lord Bute. Architect Sir William Chambers built the Pagoda, Orangery, Ruined Arch and three temples. Later, George III enlarged the gardens and Sir Joseph Banks (head gardener 1772–1819) planted them with specimens from all over the world.

Victorian order When the gardens were given to the nation in 1841, Sir William Hooker became director. He founded the Department of Economic Botany, the museums, the Herbarium and the Library, while W. A. Nesfield laid out the lake, pond and the four great vistas: Pagoda Vista, Broad Walk, Holly Walk and Cedar Vista.

The greenhouses Chambers' Orangery (1761) is now a shop and restaurant. Decimus Burton designed the Palm House (1844–48) and Temperate House (1860–62), which preserves some plants that are extinct in their countries of origin. See too Waterlily House (1852) and the Princess of Wales Conservatory (1987).

More to See

BRITISH LIBRARY

www.bl.uk

Colin St. John Wilson's redbrick home (1998) for the nation's books, with public galleries and piazza.

➕ J1 ✉ 96 Euston Road, NW1 ☎ 0870 444 1500 🕐 Mon–Fri 9.30–6, Tue 9.30–8, Sat 9.30–5, Sun 11–5 🍽 Café, restaurant 🚇 Kings Cross 💰 Donation

CANARY WHARF

César Pelli's soaring, pyramid-topped tower (1991) dominates Canary Wharf.

➕ Off map at S5 ✉ 1 Canada Square, Canary Wharf, Isle of Dogs, E14 🕐 Public spaces are open, not buildings 🚇 Canary Wharf

CHELSEA PHYSIC GARDEN

www.chelseaphysicgarden.co.uk

Charming alled garden laid out in 1673 by Sir Hans Sloane for the Society of Apothecaries.

➕ Off map at C9 ✉ 66 Royal Hospital Road, SW3 ☎ 020 7352 5646 🕐 Mid-Mar to end Oct Wed 12–5, Sun 2–6 🚇 Sloane Square 💰 Moderate

CHISWICK HOUSE

www.chgt.org.uk

Lord Burlington's exquisite country villa (1725–29), whose formal garden is an integral part of his design.

➕ Off map at A9 ✉ Burlington Lane, W4 ☎ 020 8995 0508 🕐 Apr–end Oct Sun, Wed–Fri 10–5, Sat 10–2; Nov–end Dec pre-booked tours only 🍽 Café 🚇 Turnham Green 🚉 Chiswick 💰 Moderate

DULWICH PICTURE GALLERY

www.dulwichpicturegallery.org.uk

Opened in 1814, this was England's first public art gallery.

➕ Off map at N9 ✉ Gallery Road, SE21 ☎ 020 8693 5254 🕐 Tue–Fri 10–5, Sat–Mon 11–5 🍽 Café 🚉 North or West Dulwich 💰 Moderate

FIREPOWER MUSEUM

www.firepower.org.uk

The Royal Artillery collections in the historic Royal Arsenal, ranging from Roman trebuchets to an Iraqi super-gun, and plenty of visitor participation.

➕ Off map at S7 ✉ The Royal Arsenal, Woolwich, SE18 ☎ 0208 8855 7755

Chiswick House, built in classical style

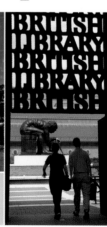

Elaborate wrought-iron doubles as the entrance to the British Library

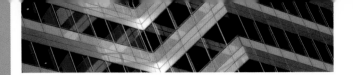

🕙 Apr–end Oct Wed–Sun 10.30–5; Nov–end Mar Fri–Sun 11–5 🚇 Woolwich Arsenal 🚢 Ferry from Greenwich 💷 Expensive

HAM HOUSE

www.nationaltrust.org.uk
Thameside baroque mansion dating from 1610; house and garden meticulously restored.
➕ Off map at A10 ✉ Ham, Richmond, Surrey ☎ 020 8940 1950 🕙 House end Mar–end Oct Sat–Wed 1–5. Gardens all year Sat–Wed 11–6 (or dusk) 🍴 Tearoom 🚇 Richmond, then bus 371 💷 Expensive

HAMPSTEAD HEATH

www.cityoflondon.gov.uk
For many north Londoners, sunny mornings on Hampstead Heath are an essential part of life.
➕ Off map at H1 ✉ 8km (5 miles) NW of Trafalgar Square ☎ 020 7482 7073 Information centre 🕙 Daily 8am–dusk 🚇 Hampstead 💷 Free

JEWISH MUSEUM

www.jewishmuseum. org.uk
One of two museums devoted to London's Jewish community (the other is in Finchley).
➕ Off map at J1 ✉ 129–131 Albert Street, NW1 ☎ 020 7284 1997 🕙 Mon–Thu 10–4, Sun 10–5 🚇 Camden Town 💷 Moderate

KENWOOD HOUSE

www.english-heritage.org.uk
Country house outside pretty Hampstead village, restyled by Robert Adam; walls are hung with Rembrandts, Romneys, Vermeers and Gainsboroughs. The gardens are now part of expansive Hampstead Heath.
➕ Off map at H1 ✉ Hampstead Lane, NW3 ☎ 020 8348 1286 🕙 Apr–end Oct daily 11–5; Nov–end Mar daily 11–4 🚇 Golders Green 💷 Free

LONDON WETLAND CENTRE

www.wwt.org.uk
The Wildfowl and Wetlands Trust administer 42ha (104 acres) of lakes, ponds, grassland and mudflats that attract an abundance of wildlife.
➕ Off map at A9 ✉ Queen Elizabeth's Walk, SW13 ☎ 020 8409 4400 🕙 Mar–end Oct daily 9.30–6; Nov–end Feb

Taking a stroll over Hampstead Heath

The stylish Jacobean Ham House

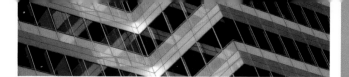

9.30–5 🚇 Hammersmith, then bus 283
🚃 Barnes then bus 33, 72 💷 Expensive

MADAME TUSSAUD'S

www.madame-tussauds.co.uk
See how many people you can identify,
from Shakespeare to Madonna. Have
an encounter with 'Big Brother' or see
if you really do have the 'X Factor'.
➕ E3 ✉ Marylebone Road, W1 ☎ 0870
400 3000 🕐 Daily 9.30–5.30 🍽 Café
🚇 Baker Street 💷 Expensive; family ticket

MUSEUM IN DOCKLANDS

www.museumindocklands.org.uk
A host of objects and displays tell the
story of London's river, port and peo-
ple from Roman times until now.
➕ Off map at S5 ✉ No. 1 Warehouses,
West India Quay, Canary Wharf, E14 ☎ 0870
444 3852 🕐 Daily 10–6 🍽 Restaurant
🚇 West India Quay 💷 Moderate

REGENT'S PARK AND ZSL LONDON ZOO

www.royalparks.org.uk; www.zsl.org
The park has vast rose gardens, a
boating lake, sports facilities and an
open-air theatre in the summer.
London Zoo is popular with children
and offers activities during holidays.
➕ Off map at D1–F1 ✉ Marleybone Road,
NW1 ☎ Park: 020 7486; zoo: 020 7722
3333 🕐 Park: daily 5am–dusk; zoo: Mar–
end Oct daily 10–5.30, Nov–end Mar daily
10–4 🍽 Cafés 🚇 Regent's Park, Camden
Town 💷 Park: free; zoo: expensive

V & A MUSEUM OF CHILDHOOD

www.vam.ac.uk/moc
An enormous train shed packed with
Noah's arks, dolls, toy soldiers and
even a model circus.
➕ Off map at S2 ✉ Cambridge Heath
Road, E2 ☎ 020 8983 5200/2415 🕐 Daily
10–5.45 🍽 Café 🚇 Bethnal Green
🚃 Bethnal Green 💷 Free

WHITECHAPEL ART GALLERY

www.whitechapel.org
The newly expanded hub of the vibrant
East End contemporary art activities.
➕ S4 ✉ 80 Whitechapel High Street, E1
☎ 020 7522 7888 🕐 Tue, Wed, Fri–Sun
11–6, Thu 11–9 🍽 Café 🚇 Aldgate East
💷 Free

Kenwood House, another good reason to visit to Hampstead Heath

Excursions

EXCURSIONS

FARTHER AFIELD

THE BASICS

www.hrp.org.uk

✉ East Molesey, Surrey

☎ 0844 482 7777

◷ End Mar–end Oct daily 10–6; Nov–end Mar daily 10–4.30

💷 Expensive

🚆 Waterloo train station to Hampton Court

🚢 Riverboat to Hampton Court

HAMPTON COURT PALACE

This is London's most impressive royal palace, well worth the trip out of the city.

When King Henry VIII dismissed Cardinal Wolsey in 1529, he took over his already ostentatious Tudor palace and enlarged it. Successive monarchs altered and repaired both the palace and its 12ha (29 acres) of Tudor and baroque gardens. The best way to visit this huge collection of chambers, courtyards and state apartments is to follow one of the six clearly indicated routes—perhaps Henry VIII's State Apartments or the King's Apartments built for William III, immaculately restored after a devastating fire. Do not miss the Tudor gardens, the Maze and restored Privy Garden, where there are guided historical walks each afternoon.

THE BASICS

www.windsor.gov.uk

ℹ Windsor Royal Station

☎ 01753 743900

◷ Oct–end Apr Mon–Sat 10–5, Sun 11–4; May–end Sep Mon–Sat 9.30–5.30, Sun 10–4

🚆 Waterloo, Paddington

Windsor Castle

☎ 020 7766 7304

◷ Mar–end Oct daily 9.45–5; Nov–end Feb 9.45–4 💷 Expensive

WINDSOR

The fairy-tale towers and turrets of Windsor Castle make this the ultimate queen's castle.

Begun by William the Conqueror and rebuilt in stone by Henry II, it has been embellished periodically. If the State Apartments and St. George's Chapel are closed, there is still plenty to see. Don't miss Queen Mary's Dolls' House designed by Edward Lutyens. Changing of the Guard is at 11am. Outside the castle lie Windsor's pretty, medieval cobblestone lanes, Christopher Wren's Guildhall and the delightful Theatre Royal. Beyond it, you can explore 1,950ha (4,700-acre) Windsor Great Park.

Greenwich Adventure

This is one of the great London outings. Revel in the sheer beauty of it all, and dip into the buildings that intrigue you (▷ 96).

DISTANCE: 5km (3 miles) **ALLOW:** One day

START

GREENWICH PIER
🚇 DLR Greenwich/Cutty Sark 🚢 Greenwich Pier

END

ISLAND GARDENS
🚇 DLR Island Gardens

❶ From Greenwich Pier walk straight ahead to the once tall-masted 1869 tea clipper, *Cutty Sark*. The tiny yacht just beyond is Sir Francis Chichester's *Gipsy Moth IV*.

❷ Return past Greenwich Pier and east along the riverside footpath. Christopher Wren's Old Royal Naval College is on the right. There are fine views from here.

❸ Proceed along the river to Park Row and the Trafalgar Tavern (a good pit-stop). Turn away from the river and go along Park Row and then cross the main road.

❹ On the right are the National Maritime Museum and Inigo Jones's royal Queen's House. Take the first path in front of Queen's House and then the next right.

❽ Back on Greenwich Church Street, go right, cross College Approach and you are back at the *Cutty Sark*. Cross under the river via the foot tunnel to Island Gardens, for views of Greenwich.

❼ Take the gravel drive on the left to Crooms Hill where the Fan Museum is at No. 12. Continue to the bottom and into Stockwell Street. Turn right into Greenwich Church Street and find the crafts market down an alley near Nelson Road.

❻ At the top cross the grass to the Royal Observatory and stand on the Greenwich Meridian. From General James Wolfe's statue walk along Blackheath Road to a roundabout. Go right and follow the path to a gate in the wall.

❺ Next, climb One Tree Hill, second path on the left, for rewarding views.

Shopping

ANTIQUARIUS
London's oldest antiques complex houses around 100 dealers whose goods include lace, old clothes and jewellery; there are plenty of quirky, affordable items.
✚ Off map ✉ 131–141 King's Road, SW3 ☎ 020 7351 5353 Ⓜ Sloane Square

BERMONDSEY MARKET
Great fun to rise before dawn and join the antiques hunters—best for small items.
✚ R8 ✉ Bermondsey Street, SE1 ☎ 020 7525 5000 Ⓜ London Bridge

BOOKS FOR COOKS
Possibly the world's best selection of books about cooking and cuisine; orders are taken and dispatched worldwide. Sample different recipes every day.
✚ Off map ✉ 4 Blenheim Crescent, W11 ☎ 020 7221 1992 Ⓜ Ladbroke Grove

BRORA
Cashmere in an array of shades for men, women and children. Located on the King's Road among some other good shops, Brora is pricey but the quality is great.
✚ Off map ✉ 344 King's Road, SW3 ☎ 020 7352 3697 Ⓜ South Kensington

CAMDEN MARKETS
The small, vibrant market in Camden Lock has expanded and spawned other markets, from the Underground station up to Hawley Road. Find crafts, clothes, books and more. Parts of the canal-side Camden Lock market were destroyed by fire in February 2008, but developers pledged to rebuild the affected areas.
✚ Off map ✉ Camden High Street to Chalk Farm Road, NW1 ◷ Daily 9.30–5.30 with more stalls on weekends Ⓜ Camden Town

CAMDEN PASSAGE
The shops stock serious antiques, the stalls are a potpourri of good, bad and fun.
✚ Off map ✉ Upper Street, N1 ☎ 020 7359 0190 ◷ Wed 7–4, Sat 7–5; books only Thu 8.30–6 Ⓜ Angel

CERAMICA BLUE
Huge collection of functional and decorative contemporary ceramic designs, made exclusively by potters worldwide.
✚ Off map ✉ 10 Blenheim Crescent, W11 ☎ 020 7727 0288 Ⓜ Ladbroke Grove, Notting Hill Gate

DAUNT BOOKS
In his panelled and stained-glass elegant 1910 shop, James Daunt keeps an impressive stock of travelogues and guides.
✚ F3 ✉ 83–84 Marylebone High Street, W1 ☎ 020 7224 2295 Ⓜ Baker Street

DESIGNER'S GUILD
Tricia Guild's store is a wonderland of exquisite design featuring a range of contemporary china, glass and fabrics.
✚ Off map ✉ 277 King's Road, SW3 ☎ 020 7351 5775 Ⓜ Sloane Square, then a 15 min walk or bus 19 or 22

DESIGNER WAREHOUSE SALES
Behind King's Cross train station, bargains galore. Seven sales a year.
✚ Off map ✉ 45 Balfe Street, N1 ☎ 020 7837 3322 Ⓜ King's Cross

ROCOCO
Delicious and imaginative chocolates—go for artisan bars flavoured with Earl Grey tea, chili pepper, nutmeg, cardamom or wild mint leaves. A taste sensation.
✚ Off map ✉ 321 King's Road, SW3 ☎ 020 7352 5857 Ⓜ Sloane Square

ONE-STOP SHOPPING
The one-stop shopping that department stores offer has several advantages over slogging around the streets. If it rains, you stay dry. If you are hungry, there are cafés. Your purchases from various departments can be held for you while you shop, to be collected together at the end. Garments can be altered, presents wrapped and writing paper printed. And most stores have dependable after-sales service if something is not right.

Entertainment and Nightlife

BARFLY
www.barflyclub.com
A Camden club that hosts more than 20 indie groups a week—some bad, some OK and some destined for stardom.
Off map ✉ 49 Chalk Farm Road, NW1 ☎ 020 7691 4244 🚇 Chalk Farm

BOSTON ARMS
www.dirtywaterclub.com
A variety of music at this fashionable pub in North London's Tufnell Park.
Off map ✉ 178 Junction Road, N19 ☎ 07786 805518 🚇 Tufnell Park

BULL'S HEAD, BARNES
www.thebullshead.com
Good jazz in the friendly village atmosphere of a riverside pub.
Off map ✉ 373 Lonsdale Road, SW13 ☎ 020 8876 5241 🚇 Barnes Bridge

CANVAS
www.canvaslondon.net
One of a cluster of King's Cross clubs with a huge space. Music and dress style varies each night.
K1 ✉ King's Cross Goods Yard, off York Way, N1 ☎ 0845 371 4489 🚇 King's Cross

JAZZ CAFÉ
www.meanfiddler.com
Popular riverside spot for the young; buzzes nightly with the widest range of jazz, from soul to rap.
Off map ✉ 5 Parkway, NW1 ☎ 020 7534 6955 (restaurant); 0870 060 37787 (tickets) 🚇 Camden Town

THE O₂ ARENA
www.theO2.co.uk
Music and sports venue in former Millennium Dome, with a capacity of 20,000.
Off map ✉ Peninsula Square, SE10 ☎ 0871 984 0002 🚇 North Greenwich

SADLER'S WELLS THEATRE
www.sadlerswells.com
The most electrifying dance theatre in Europe, newly built for 2000—a must for all ballet fans.
M1 ✉ Rosebery Avenue, EC1 ☎ 020 7863 8000 🚇 Angel

SCALA
www.scala-london.co.uk
Another King's Cross superclub, spread over three floors with a viewing gallery.
Off map ✉ King's Cross, N1 ☎ 020 7833 2022 🚇 King's Cross

PUB MUSIC
This can be one of the least expensive and most enjoyable evenings out in London, worth the trip to an off-beat location. For the price of a pint of beer (usually a huge choice) you can settle down to enjoy the ambience and listen to some of the best alternative music available in town—from folk, jazz and blues to rhythm and blues, soul and more. Audiences tend to be friendly, loyal to their venue and happy to talk music.

Sport
ALL ENGLAND LAWN TENNIS CLUB, WIMBLEDON
www.wimbledon.org
Tennis's top tournament starts here late June. Enter the ticket ballot or line up for tickets, except on the last four days.
Off map ✉ Church Road, SW19 ☎ 020 8946 2244 🚇 Southfields

BRIT OVAL
www.surreycricket.com
Surrey home games and test cricket; also Sunday league games.
Off map ✉ Surrey County Cricket Club, The Oval, SE11 ☎ 08712 461100 🚇 Oval

LORD'S CRICKET GROUND
www.lords.org
Home of the MCC (Marylebone Cricket Club); watch Middlesex play home games, test cricket, major finals and Sunday league games.
Off map ✉ St. John's Wood Road, NW8 ☎ 020 7616 8500 🚇 St. John's Wood

WEMBLEY
www.wembleystadium.com
www.livenation.co.uk/wembley
The Arena for boxing, snooker, show-jumping and more. The 2006 state-of-the art stadium for football.
Off map ✉ Stadium Way, Wembley, Middx ☎ 0844 800 2755 🚇 Wembley Park 🚉 Wembley Stadium

Restaurants

PRICES

Prices are approximate, based on a 3-course meal for one person.

£££   over £60
££   £30–£60
£   under £30

BABYLON (££)

www.roofgardens.com
Virgin supremo Richard Branson has revived this eccentric rooftop venue, complete with trees and pink flamingos. Good brasserie food.
➕ Off map ✉ The Roof Garden, 99 Kensington High Street, W8 ☎ 020 7368 3993 🕐 Mon–Sat 12–3, 7–11 🚇 Farringdon

BIG CHILL BAR (£)

www.bigchill.net
Historic building offering space, good food, music and summer festivals.
➕ S3 ✉ Brick Lane, E1 ☎ 020 7392 9180 🕐 Mon–Sat noon–late, Sun 12–11.30pm 🚇 Aldgate East

LE CAFÉ ANGLAIS (£)

Rowley Leigh's new venture, this vast but inviting art deco restaurant in the Whiteley's shopping centre attracts food-lovers with an unfussy menu and an open kitchen.
➕ A4 ✉ 8 Porchester Gardens, W2 ☎ 020 7221 1415 🕐 Daily 12–3, 6.30–11 🚇 Bayswater

FIFTEEN (££)

www.fifteen.net
Successful training for the unemployed. Jamie Oliver's mainly Italian cuisine means there are plenty of good choices.
➕ Q1 ✉ 15 Westland Place, N1 ☎ 0871 330 1515 🕐 Mon–Sat 7.30–11, 12–3, 6.30–9.45, Sun 8–11, 12–3.30, 6.30–9.45 🚇 Old Street

THE GLASSHOUSE (££)

www.glasshouserestaurant.co.uk
The perfect preamble to a walk in Kew Gardens. Reserve to enjoy notable modern dishes. Right next to Kew station.
➕ Off map ✉ 14 Station Parade, Kew ☎ 020 8940 6777 🕐 Mon–Thu 12–2.30, 7–10.30, Fri–Sat 12–2.30, 6.30–10.30, Sun 12.30–3, 7–10 🚇 Kew Gardens

GUN (££)

www.thegundocklands.com
Popular, comfortable gastropub on Canary Wharf, with stunning views.
➕ Off map ✉ 27 Coldharbour, Isle of Dogs, E14 ☎ 020 7515 5222 🕐 Mon–Sat 11am–midnight, Sun 11–11 🚇 Old Street

BUFFET DEALS

Unlimited food at a fixed price is practical for families with growing children–or simply for hungry adults. Many larger hotels do breakfast and lunch buffets, especially good on Sunday when many Indian restaurants do the same–the Conrad Hotel's luxurious buffet is legendary.

MEDCALF (££)

www.medcalfbar.co.uk
Informal, with music at night, yet a carefully crafted menu that respects top-quality ingredients.
➕ M2 ✉ 40 Exmouth Market, EC1 ☎ 020 7833 3533 🕐 Mon–Thu 12–3, 6–9.45, Fri–Sat 12–3, 6–10.15, Sun 12–4 🚇 Farringdon

OTTOLENGHI (£)

Merely looking at the restaurant is sustaining; eating here is even better.
➕ Off map ✉ 287 Upper Street, N1 ☎ 020 7288 1454 🕐 Mon–Sat 8am–11pm, Sun 9am–7pm 🚇 Angel, Highbury, Islington

PROVIDORES & TAPA ROOM (££)

www.theprovidores.co.uk
Peter Gordon uses a true knowledge of world cuisines to let his imagination fly.
➕ F3 ✉ 109 Marylebone High Street, W1 ☎ 020 7935 6175 🕐 Mon–Sat 12–2.45, 6–10.30, Sun 12–2.45, 6–10 🚇 Baker Street

VILLANDRY (££)

www.villandry.com
Marylebone, north of Oxford Street, has some fantastic eateries and Villandry, with its simple but tasty specialties, is no exception. There's a delicatessen too. Live jazz in the bar on Saturday nights.
➕ G3 ✉ 170 Greata Portland Street, W1W ☎ 020 7631 3131 🕐 Mon–Sat 12–3, 6–10.30, Sun 11.30–4 🚇 Baker Street

FARTHER AFIELD | **'RESTAURANTS**

It can never be said too often: London is huge, so where you stay is all to do with location. Next truth: London accommodation is expensive. Find somewhere that suits your budget and your style, then fight for the best deal.

Introduction	**108**
Budget Hotels	**109**
Mid-Range Hotels	**110–111**
Luxury Hotels	**112**

Introduction

London has some of the best hotels in the world, but the cost of accommodation is high. You can expect to pay £150 a night for a reasonable room, and the rates begin to soar if you stay at one of the grand old hotels such as the Dorchester or the Savoy.

Booking

Many hotels will ask you to confirm your reservation and will charge a fee if you cancel at short notice or fail to turn up. You may lose your deposit or even have two nights charged to your credit card. Most hotels have rooms of different sizes, so always ask whether there is a choice. You will not necessarily be allocated the best room available. Good value hotels and guesthouses do exist, but these rooms are very much in demand and you must reserve in advance.

Tight Budget

Consider alternatives to hotels, such as renting an apartment, staying in a bed-and-breakfast or staying with a London family (for information consult www.bedandbreakfast.com or the London Tourist website). Even cheaper, consider a youth hostel (Youth Hostel Association (☎ 0870 770 8868, +44 1629 592700 from outside UK; reservations 0870 770 6113, +44 1629 592708 from outside UK; www.yha. org.uk). Membership is required; you can join in advance or at any hostel. Many hotels offer bargain rates on weekends and during February, March, October and November. You can almost always avoid paying full price.

NOISE LEVELS

The biggest problem with London hotels is noise, and many are on busy streets. Some have double glazing, but that can make rooms unbearably stuffy, especially since air-conditioning is not standard. If you value peace and quiet, look for hotels on side streets in residential areas; or request a room at the rear of or higher up in the building.

From grand and luxurious to the more modest, bed and breakfast and hostels, London can provide it all

Budget Hotels

PRICES

Expect to pay under £100 per night for a budget hotel

ASHLEE HOUSE

www.ashleehouse.co.uk
Funky youth hostel; a great location for King's Cross clubbing. 170 beds in 33 rooms.
➕ K1 ✉ 261–265 Gray's Inn Road, WC1 ☎ 020 7833 9400, fax 0207833 9677
Ⓔ King's Cross

EASYHOTEL

www.easyhotel.com
Inexpensive but basic in the extreme; few rooms have windows. 80 rooms.
➕ A8 ✉ 14 Lexham Gardens, W8 ☎ Reserve by website only Ⓔ Earl's Court, Gloucester Road

GENERATOR

www.the-generator.co.uk
This stylish, industrial-style building offers 800 guests bunk-bedded rooms and excellent facilities. Party atmosphere. 217 rooms.
➕ K2 ✉ Compton Place, Tavistock Place, WC1 ☎ 020 7388 7666, fax 020 7388 7644
Ⓔ Russell Square

INTERNATIONAL STUDENTS HOUSE

www.ish.org.uk
Rooms and family flats by Regent's Park. Reserve well ahead. 304 rooms.
➕ G3 ✉ 229 Great Portland Street, W1 ☎ 020 7631 8300, fax 020 7631 8315 Ⓔ Great Portland Street, Regent's Park

KENSINGTON MANOR

www.kensingtonmanorhotel.co.uk
Well-placed for South Kensington museums and Knightsbridge shopping. 14 rooms.
➕ A8 ✉ 8 Emperors Gate, SW7 ☎ 020 7370 7516, fax 020 7373 3163
Ⓔ Gloucester Road

MORGAN

www.morganhotel.co.uk
Renovated, family-run, friendly and well-located. The Morgan has just 20 rooms, so book ahead.
➕ J3 ✉ 24 Bloomsbury Street, WC1 ☎ 020 7636 3735, fax 020 7636 3045
Ⓔ Tottenham Court Road

PAVILION HOTEL

www.pavilionhoteluk.com
Plain façade belies witty fantasy decor inside. 30 rooms.
➕ C4 ✉ 34–36 Sussex Gardens, W2 ☎ 020 7262 0905, fax 020 7262 1324
Ⓔ Paddington

LOCATION

It is well worth perusing the London map to decide where you are likely to spend most of your time. Then select a hotel in that area or accessible to it by Underground on a direct line, so you avoid having to change trains. London is vast and it takes time to cross, particularly by bus and costly taxis. By paying a little more to be in the heart of the city, you will save on travel time and costs.

PREMIER INN CAPITAL

www.premierinn.com
Practical, no-frills chain whose star London location is in County Hall, opposite the Houses of Parliament. 313 rooms.
➕ L7 ✉ County Hall, Belvedere Road, SE1 ☎ 0870 238 3300, fax 020 7902 1619
Ⓔ Waterloo

TRAVELODGE

www.travelodge.co.uk
Located in a quiet spot not far from Liverpool Street Station, this hotel provides 142 adequate rooms at good rates. Ideal for families.
➕ R4 ✉ 1 Harrow Place, E1 ☎ 0870 191 1689
Ⓔ Liverpool Street

22 YORK STREET

www.22yorkstreet.co.uk
Elegant Georgian homes transformed into quality B&B. 20 rooms.
➕ E3 ✉ 22 York Street, W1 ☎ 020 7224 2990, fax 020 7224 1990 Ⓔ Baker Street

UNIVERSITY WOMEN'S CLUB

www.universitywomensclub.com
In an old Mayfair house; membership open to all women graduates and similarly qualified women; friends pay a temporary membership fee. 24 rooms.
➕ F6 ✉ 2 Audley Square, South Audley Street, W1 ☎ 020 7499 2268, fax 020 7499 7046 Ⓔ Hyde Park Corner

Mid-Range Hotels

PRICES

Expect to pay between £100 and £250 per night for a mid-range hotel

ACADEMY
www.theetoncollection.com
Excellent location for the British Museum. Set in five converted Georgian town houses with exceptionally light, modern rooms. 50 rooms.
🔹 J3 ✉ 21 Gower Street, WC1 ☎ 020 7631 4115, fax 020 7636 3442
🔘 Goodge Street

ASTER HOUSE
www.asterhouse.com
Standing with other chic B&Bs in a smart South Kensington stuccoed terrace, you can enjoy the garden, palm-filled conservatory, power showers and nearby museums.
🔹 C9 ✉ 3 Sumner Place, SW3 ☎ 020 7581 5888, fax 020 7584 4925 🔘 South Kensington

BERJAYA EDEN PARK
www.berjayaresorts. com
An elegant 1860 Bayswater town house, on a tree-lined terrace. Rooms are simple. Public rooms include a restaurant and bar. 15 rooms.
🔹 A5 ✉ 35–39 Inverness Terrace, W2 ☎ 020 7221 2220, fax 020 7221 2286
🔘 Bayswater

BLAKES
www.blakeshotels.com
Sumptuous decadence achieved by designer Anoushka Hempel. 51 rooms.
🔹 Off map ✉ 33 Roland Gardens, SW7 ☎ 020 7370 6701, fax 020 7373 0442
🔘 South Kensington

CHAMBERLAIN
www.fullershotels.com
Lavishly converted from 20th-century offices, this hotel is ideally situated for visiting the city's attractions. The 64 bedrooms are stylish and have modern bathrooms. There is a popular pub is on the premises.
🔹 S4 ✉ 130–135 Minories, EC3 ☎ 020 7680 1500, fax 020 7702 2500
🔘 Fenchurch Street

CHARLOTTE STREET HOTEL
www.firmdale.com
Kit and Tim Kemp's boutique cocktail of serious comfort and fairy-tale Englishness with 52 rooms.
🔹 H3 ✉ 15 Charlotte

HIDDEN COSTS

The room price quoted by a hotel may, or may not, include continental breakfast or full English breakfast and VAT, which is currently 17.5 per cent. Since these affect the final bill dramatically, it is vital to ask in advance. Check the percentage markup on telephone and internet connection, and business office facilities and ask about the laundry service, which can be very slow.

Street, W1 ☎ 020 7806 2000, fax 020 7806 2002
🔘 Goodge Street

COVENT GARDEN HOTEL
www.firmdale.com
Another of Kit Kemp's stylish boutique hotels, this one attracts film stars who enjoy its 58 traditional yet contemporary British rooms, bathrooms and library.
🔹 J4 ✉ 10 Monmouth Street, WC2 ☎ 020 7806 1000, fax 020 7806 1100
🔘 Leicester Square

GORING
www.goringhotel.co.uk
High standards of old-fashioned hospitality and service make this splendid hotel memorable. Owned by the Goring family for almost a century. There are 74 stylish rooms and the smart reception rooms have been renovated by David Linley.
🔹 G8 ✉ Beeston Place, Grosvenor Gardens, SW1 ☎ 020 7396 9000, fax 020 7834 4393 🔘 Victoria

KENSINGTON HOUSE
www.kenhouse.com
Beautiful restored 19th-century property providing contemporary accommodation in the heart of Kensington. The 41 bedrooms are light and stylish.
🔹 A7 ✉ 15–16 Prince of Wales Terrace, W8 ☎ 020 7937 2345, fax 020 7368 6700
🔘 High Street Kensington

THE LEONARD

www.theleonard.com
Discreet, small hotel, near
Oxford Street; comfortable, superbly decorated
bedrooms. 28 rooms.
 E4 ✉ 15 Seymour Street,
W1 ☎ 020 7935 2010, fax
020 7935 6700 Ⓜ Marble
Arch

MALMAISON

www.malmaison.com
In atmospheric
Clerkenwell, yet totally
contemporary in providing what guests need.
97 rooms.
🞦 N3 ✉ Charterhouse
Square, EC1 ☎ 020 7012
3700, fax 020 7012 3702
Ⓜ Farringdon

THE MANDEVILLE

www.mandeville.co.uk
Kitsch yet contemporary,
in an elegant Edwardian
building a short stroll
from Oxford Street.
Colourful fun bars and
restaurants.166 rooms.
🞦 F4 ✉ Mandeville Place,
W1U ☎ 020 7955 5599, fax
020 7706 1028 Ⓜ Bond Street

MORNINGTON HOTEL

www.bestwestern.co.uk
Comfortable up-to-date
accommodation in a fine
Victorian building. On a
quiet road close to an
Underground service to
the West End.
🞦 C5 ✉ 12 Lancaster Gate,
W2 ☎ 020 7262 7361, fax
020 7706 1028 Ⓜ Bond Street

PORTOBELLO

www.portobello-hotel.co.uk
Romantic retreat with
exotic, sumptuous rooms,
close to the antiques
shops of Portobello Road.
24 rooms.
🞦 Off map ✉ 22 Stanley
Gardens, W11 ☎ 020 7727
2777, fax 020 7792 9641
Ⓜ Notting Hill Gate

ROOKERY

www.rookeryhotel.co.uk
Enjoy discreet comforts
in this wonderfully atmospheric small hotel,
enhanced with antiques,
open fires and Victorian
bathrooms. 33 rooms.
🞦 N3 ✉ Cowcross Street,
EC1 ☎ 020 7336 0931,
fax 020 7336 0932
Ⓜ Farringdon

SOUTHWARK ROSE

www.southwarkrosehotel.co.uk
Great location for the Tate
Modern and, via the
Millennium Bridge, the

MODERN HOTELS

London has many contemporary hotels, from starkly minimal to sumptuously luxurious.
At the top end, try the Andaz
Hotel (▷ 112) and Kit
Kemp's six London hotels
(www.firmdalecom). In the
mid-range try Schrager's
Sanderson (✉ 50 Berners
Street, W1 ☎ 020 7300 1400;
www.sandersonhotels.com),
No. 5 Maddox Street (✉ 5
Maddox Street, W1 ☎ 020
7647 0200; www.living-rooms.co.uk) or myhotel
Bloomsbury (✉ 11–13
Bayley Street, Bedford
Square, W1 ☎ 020 7667
6000; www.myhotels.co.uk).

rest of Central London.
Contemporary, chic;
notable family suites with
kitchenettes.
🞦 P6 ✉ 43–47 Southwark
Bridge Road, SE1 ☎ 020
7015 1480, fax 020 7015 1481
Ⓜ London Bridge

THE TRAFALGAR

www.hilton.co.uk
Hard to beat this boutique hotel for its central
location, congenial buzzy
atmosphere, classy cocktails and smart but simple
rooms. 129 rooms.
🞦 J6 ✉ 2 Spring Gardens,
SW1 ☎ 020 7970 2900,
fax 020 7870 2911 Ⓜ Charing
Cross

VANCOUVER STUDIOS

www.vancouverstudios.co.uk
Deep in West London, on
Notting Hill's trendy
doorstep, these clean,
comfortable studios are
each fitted with a mini-kitchen making them
super value for money.
Interior is funky as well as
functional. A new garden
apartment sleeps six for
extra economy.
🞦 Off map ✉ 20 Prince's
Square, Bayswater, W2
☎ 020 7243 1270, fax 020
7221 8678 Ⓜ Bayswater

ZETTER ROOMS

www.thezetter.com
Hip contemporary hotel
in Clerkenwell, with
restaurant and bar to
match. Great views from
rooftop suites. 59 rooms.
🞦 N2 ✉ 86–88 Clerkenwell
Road, EC1 ☎ 020 7324 4444,
fax 020 7324 4445
Ⓜ Farringdon

Luxury Hotels

PRICES

Expect to pay over £250 per night for a luxury hotel

ANDAZ

www.london.liverpoolstreet.andaz.com
Casual luxury is the theme of this Hyatt-owned hotel in a converted Victorian railway hotel.
 R3 ✉ 40 Liverpool Street, EC2 ☎ 020 7618 5000, fax 020 7618 5001 Ⓠ Liverpool Street

BERKELEY

www.theberkeleyhotellondon.com
A change of hotel group and a refurbishment has kept this hotel up to pace for business and pleasure. Health spa, rooftop pool and two restaurants.
🔟 E7 ✉ Wilton Square, SW1 ☎ 020 7235 6000, fax 020 7235 4430 Ⓠ Hyde Park Corner

DORCHESTER

www.dorchesterhotel.com
One of London's finest hotels. Deliciously art deco, a London landmark from its grand entrance and piano bar to the Oliver Messel suite. Some 250 bedrooms have huge, luxury bathrooms.
🔟 F6 ✉ Park Lane, W1 ☎ 020 7629 8888, fax 020 7409 0114 Ⓠ Green Park, Hyde Park Corner

HALKIN HOTEL

www.halkin.como.bz
Central London's first boutique hotel has been renovated, blending western and Asian aesthetics. Good Thai restaurant. 41 rooms.
🔟 F7 ✉ 4 Halkin Street, SW1 ☎ 020 7333 1000, fax 020 7333 1100 Ⓠ Hyde Park Corner

HAZLITT'S

www.hazlittshotel.com
Near-perfect period decoration in three 18th-century houses; superb location for theatres. 23 rooms.
🔟 J4 ✉ 6 Frith Street, W1 ☎ 020 7434 1771, fax 020 7430 1524 Ⓠ Tottenham Court Road

ONE ALDWYCH

www.onealdwych.com
This stylish contemporary hotel in an Edwardian building epitomizes London's current hotel fashion for restrained luxury. 105 rooms.

BARGAIN LUXURY

To be pampered amid sumptuous surroundings may be an essential part of your trip. London's most luxurious hotels have been built with no expense spared. Hotel prices are generally very high, but quality rooms can be had for bargain prices. It's always worth asking when you make your reservation whether any special deals are available. Most deluxe and mid-range hotels offer weekend deals throughout the year.

🔟 L5 ✉ 1 Aldwych, WC2 ☎ 020 7300 1000, fax 020 7300 1001 Ⓠ Covent Garden, Temple

THE RITZ

www.theritzlondon.com
Small but sumptuous, with plenty of old style, gilt decor and the great first-floor promenade to London's most beautiful dining room, overlooking Green Park. 133 rooms.
🔟 G6 ✉ 150 Piccadilly, W1 ☎ 020 7493 8181, fax 020 7493 2687 Ⓠ Green Park

ST. MARTIN'S LANE

www.stmartinslane.com
Theatrical minimalism at Ian Schrager and Philippe Starck's fab hotel. 204 rooms.
🔟 J5 ✉ St. Martin's Lane, WC2 ☎ 020 7300 5500, fax 020 77300 5501 Ⓠ Covent Garden, Leicester Square

SAVOY

www.savoygroup.com
A top-to-toe revamp in 2008 has brought this grand hotel into the 21st century.
🔟 L5 ✉ Strand, WC2 ☎ 020 7836 4343, fax 020 7240 6040 Ⓠ Covent Garden

SOHO HOTEL

www.sohohotel.com
Kit Kemp's latest London hotel, newly built, restrained boutique style. Locals love the public rooms. 91 rooms.
🔟 J4 ✉ 4 Richmond Mews, W1 ☎ 020 7559 3000, fax 020 7559 3003 Ⓠ Tottenham Court Road

Need to Know

Use this key information before and during your trip to check out when your kind of festival takes place, explore London web-sites and find out what you can book in advance to save money. And be sure to get savvy about public transport.

Planning Ahead	**114–115**
Getting There	**116–117**
Getting Around	**118–119**
Essential Facts	**120–123**
Timeline	**124–125**

Planning Ahead

When to Go

The tourist season is year-round, and most attractions remain open all year. Peak season is from June to September, when you should arrive with a hotel reservation and theatre tickets. The quietest months are February, March, October and November, when hotels may give a discount.

TIME

GMT (Greenwich Mean Time) is standard. BST (British Summer Time) is 1 hour ahead (late Mar–late Oct).

AVERAGE DAILY MAXIMUM TEMPERATURES

JAN	FEB	MAR	APR	MAY	JUN	JUL	AUG	SEP	OCT	NOV	DEC
42°F	45°F	50°F	55°F	63°F	68°F	72°F	72°F	66°F	57°F	50°F	45°F
6°C	7°C	10°C	13°C	17°C	20°C	22°C	22°C	19°C	14°C	10°C	7°C

Spring (March to May) has a mixture of sunshine and showers, although winter often encroaches on it.

Summer (June to August) can be unpredictable, with clear skies and searing heat one day followed by sultry greyness and thunderstorms the next.

Autumn (September to November) has clear skies that can feel almost summery. Real autumn starts in October, and colder weather sets in during November.

Winter (December to February) is generally mild, with the odd cold snap, and snow is uncommon.

WHAT'S ON

January *Sales:* Shopping bargains at stores all over the city.

February *Chinese New Year:* Dragon dances and fireworks in Soho.

March *Chelsea Antiques Fair:* Chelsea Old Town Hall.

April *Oxford and Cambridge Boat Race* (1st Sat): This famous annual race takes place on the Thames from Putney to Mortlake.

London Marathon: The world's biggest running race.

May *Chelsea Flower Show* (end of May): One of the world's best takes place at the Royal Hospital, Chelsea.

June *Trooping the Colour* (2nd Sat): The 'Colours' (flags) are trooped before the Queen on Horseguards Parade, Whitehall.

Wimbledon (Jun/Jul): The world's leading grass tennis tournament.

July *Promenade Concerts* (Jul–Aug): Nightly world-class classical concerts in the Albert Hall.

August *Notting Hill Carnival* (last weekend, Bank Holiday Monday): Europe's biggest carnival.

September *Mayor's Thames Festival:* A weekend of celebrations and fireworks to mark the mayor of London's election.

October *Pearly Kings and Queens* (1st Sun): Service at St. Martin-in-the-Fields.

November *Bonfire Night* (5 Nov): Fires and fireworks commemorate the failed Gunpowder Plot of 1605.

State Opening of Parliament: Royal procession from Buckingham Palace to the Houses of Parliament.

December *Christmas music* (all month): Christmas music fills London's churches.

Useful Websites

www.visitlondon.com
London's official site is up-to-date and comprehensive with ideas for museums, theatre and restaurants, and sections for children and visitors with disabilities. It offers discounts, too.

www.royalparks.org.uk
From Greenwich to Green Park, all eight Royal Parks are detailed here, incluoding special events and activities for children

www.tfl.gov.uk
London Transport's official site gives ideas for what to see and do, ticket information for the Underground, buses, DLR and river services. It also has a WAP-enabled journey planner.

www.royal.gov.uk
The official site of the British royal family, with history, royal residences, who's doing what today and a monthly online magazine.

www.bhrc.co.uk
The British Hotel Reservation Centre website takes bookings, from bed-and-breakfasts to grand hotels. Includes special discounts.

www.londonpass.com
On this site you can buy the London Pass card valid for 3 or 6 days, with unlimited access to more than 50 London attractions and deals on public transport.

www.hrp.org.uk
London's five great historic palaces, from the Tower of London to Hampton Court.

www.officiallondontheatre.com
The Society of London Theatre's official site, with all the latest theatre news, together with comprehensive interviews with stars, performance details and theatre access for people with disabilities.

PRIME TRAVEL SITES

www.nationaltrust.org.uk
This independent organization owns and maintains many buildings and extensive lands, some of them in and around London.

www.english-heritage.org.uk/London
English Heritage are responsible for many historic sites and buildings—many are in London.

www.fodors.com
A complete travel-planning site. You can research prices and weather; book air tickets, cars and rooms; pose questions (and get answers) from fellow travellers; and find links to other sites.

INTERNET ACCESS

easyInternetcafé
(easyEverything.com): The international chain started in London is open seven days a week and has branches throughout the city. The one at 160–166 Kensington High Street has almost 400 terminals.
Public libraries, Virgin stores and others have internet facilities. Wireless is available at Starbucks cafés, major train stations and airports. Most hotels have modem plug-in-points (data ports) in each room.

Getting There

AIRPORT TIP

To avoid the overloaded Heathrow airport year-round, and Luton at holiday periods, consider flying into Stansted for a slightly quieter and congenial arrival and departure. The train station is inside the airport terminal.

TRAINS

● For all information ☎ 08457 484950; www.nationalrail.co.uk
● Purchase tickets at the railway station or on www.thetrainline.com.
● All major London train stations are on Tube lines.
● There are eight major London train stations; sometimes a town is served by more than one (eg., Paddington and Waterloo serve Windsor).
● Fares are highly priced but there are lots of cheap deals if you book in advance and can be flexible about the time you travel.

AIRPORTS

Heathrow and Gatwick are the principal airports serving the city. However, Stansted, Luton and London City are becoming increasingly busy with traffic from Continental Europe. There are train links to the continent via Lille and Paris and road links to Channel ports.

60km (40 miles)

Luton Airport
Bus 1hr 30min; £10.50 single, £12.50 return

Stansted Airport
Bus 1hr 40min; £10 single, £17 return

City Airport
Bus 25–40mins; £from £2 single

Heathrow Airport
Bus 1hr 45min; £2–10 single, £15 return

Gatwick Airport
Bus 1hr 30min–2hr 45 min; £6.60 single, £8.80 return

FROM HEATHROW

Heathrow (☎ 0870 000 0123; www.heathrow airport.com) has five terminals, some 24km (15 miles) west of central London; all are well served by public transport. The Underground Piccadilly line runs 5am–midnight (6am–1pm Sunday); and takes about an hour. The Heathrow Express (☎ 0845 600 1515; www.heathrowexpress. co.uk), a high-speed rail link to Paddington station, runs from 5.10am–midnight every 15 minutes. Ticket prices are high for the 15-minute journey. National Express (☎ 08717 818181) buses run 5.30am–10.15pm but the trip can take more than an hour. Taxis wait outside any terminal; the trip takes about one hour—depending on the traffic; taxis cost around £60.

FROM GATWICK

Gatwick airport (☎ 0870 000 2468; www.gatwickairport.com) is 48km (30 miles) south of the heart of the city. The best way to reach London is by train: The Gatwick Express (☎ 0845 850 1530; www.gatwickexpress. com) train leaves for Victoria Station every

15 minutes, (5am–1am) and takes 30 minutes. Connex runs slightly slower but cheaper services; and Thameslink leads direct to the City and King's Cross. Taxis cost more than £100.

FROM STANSTED

Stansted airport (☎ 0870 000 0303; www. stanstedairport.com) is 56km (35 miles) northeast of central London. The Stansted Express (☎ 0845 600 7245; www.stansted express.com) to Liverpool Street Station takes around 40 minutes. Airbus A6 (☎ 0870 580 8080) runs 24 hours and takes up to 1 hour 40 minutes. A taxi costs around £100.

FROM LUTON AIRPORT

Luton airport (☎ 01582 405 100; www. london-luton.com) is 53km (33 miles) north of London. There are bus links to Victoria Coach Station, taking around 1 hour 30 minutes and Thameslink trains to King's Cross, which take 40 minutes. Taxis cost about £80.

FROM LONDON CITY AIRPORT

City Airport (☎ 020 7646 0000; www. londoncityairport.com) is at Royal Albert Docks, 9 miles (14km) east of central London. The Airport Shuttle Bus runs to Liverpool Street station; bus 473 connects to the DLR (Docklands Light Railway) station Prince Regent. Taxis wait outside the terminal and cost around £24.

THE CHANNEL TUNNEL

Eurostar (☎ 08705 186186; www.eurostar.com) connects Britain to Continental Europe. Great for arriving in London, plus trips out to Paris, Brussels and elsewhere. Book ahead for cheap deals. Trains use St. Pancras International Terminal, close to King's Cross. Eurotunnel (☎ www. eurotunnel.com) is for vehicles only. Fares are lower if you reserve ahead.

FROM THE FERRY PORTS

Various ferry companies operate services between British ports and ports in Europe.

BY COACH

If you travel to London by long-distance coach you will probably arrive at Victoria Coach Station (VCS) on Buckingham Palace Road, near Victoria main train station. The coach station is a few minutes' walk from the Underground station, which is on the Victoria, District and Circle lines. Alternatively, there is a taxi rank immediately outside VCS.

LOST/STOLEN PROPERTY

The most seasoned traveller occasionally leaves something behind—airlines find forgotten computers almost daily.

● Contact the place where you think you left it or saw it last.

● Report the loss to a police station and get a copy of the report form for your insurance claim.

● If you lose a passport, report it to the police and your embassy. Provided you have photocopies of the key pages, it should not be difficult to replace.

● Contact for London Transport and taxi lost property ☎ 0845 330 9882; www.tfl.gov.uk

Getting Around

NEED TO KNOW GETTING AROUND

DRIVING TIP

Driving in London is slow, parking is expensive and fines are high. Congestion charges operate from Monday to Friday, 7am–6pm, costing £8 a day. Do not drive in London unless you have to: use public transport.

VISITORS WITH DISABILITIES

London is steadily improving its facilities for visitors with disabilities, from shops and theatres to hotels and museums. The Government is introducing free admission for those with disabilities. Newer attractions such as Tate Modern and the London Eye are better equipped than ancient buildings such as Westminster Abbey. Check out the London Tourist Board's comprehensive website www.londontouristboard. com and guide books, such as *Access in London* (published by Access Project PHSP ☎ 39 Bradley Gardens, W13; www. accessinlondon.org). Also consult Artsline (www. artsline.org.uk), Can Be Done (www.canbedone. co.uk) and Dial (www.ldaf. org). William Forrester, a lecturer and wheelchair user, leads tailor-made tours in the city (☎ 01483 575401).

The Underground trains (known as the Tube) and buses run from around 5.30am to just after midnight, when service is via a night bus. The transport system is divided into zones—six for the Underground and four for buses—and you must have a ticket valid for the zone you are in. If you anticipate more than one journey, buy a travelcard, which allows unlimited use of the Underground, buses and Docklands Light Railway (DLR) services (▷ 119). Further information on Tube and bus ☎ 020 7222 1234; www.thetube.com; www.tfl.gov.uk.

THE UNDERGROUND (TUBE)

Twelve colour-coded lines link almost 300 stations. Use a travel pass or buy a ticket from a machine (some give change) or ticket booth; keep the ticket until the end of the journey. The system includes the Docklands Light Railway (DLR).

BUSES

Plan your journey using the latest copy of the Central London bus guide available at London Transport information centres (▷ 119) or at www.tfl.gov.uk. A flat cash fare applies across London; otherwise use a travel pass. Have the exact change ready. A bus stop is indicated by a red sign on a metal pole displaying diagrams of each route it serves.

TAXIS

Taxis that are available for rental illuminate a yellow 'For Hire' sign on the roof. Hold out your hand to hail them beside the road. Drivers of official cabs will know the city well. They are obliged to follow the shortest route unless an alternative is agreed beforehand. A 'black cab' (now often not black but a bright colour) is licensed for up to five passengers. Meter charges increase in the evenings and at weekends. Avoid minicabs if you can as they may have no meter and possibly inadequate insurance. Black cabs can be ordered by phone: Radio Taxis ☎ 020 7272 0272; www.radiotaxis.co.uk

LONDON TRANSPORT INFORMATION CENTRES

Centres sell travel passes and provide underground and train maps, bus route maps and information on cheap tickets. They are open daily at the following stations: Heathrow Terminals 1, 2 and 3, Liverpool Street, Victoria, Euston, King's Cross, Paddington. London Transport enquiries service ☎ 020 7222 1234.

TRAVEL PASSES

Travelcards: valid after 9.30am (pay a surcharge to use earlier), for unlimited travel by Tube, railway, Docklands Light Railway and most buses are sold at travel information centres, British Rail stations, all Tube stations, and some shops. They cover travel for one day or three days; there is also a one-day family card.

Oyster prepay Smartcards: valid for seven days, a month or longer, for unlimited use on the Underground, DLR, bus Thameslink and some national rail networks.

Bus passes: most central London buses require you to have a ticket before boarding, so it is easiest to buy a one-day Bus Pass or a book of tickets called a Saver.

LONDON PASS

This is a pass to more than 50 top attractions as well as an option to travel on buses, tubes and trains. The aim of the pass is to enable you to beat the crowds lining up at selected major attractions. The pass is valid for either one, two, three or six days—multiday passes must be used on consecutive days. It offers discounts on restaurants and leisure activities. Check out www.londonpass.com for more information.

BOATING AND BIKING

Thames Clippers (www.thamesclippers.com) runs a commuter service between these piers: Savoy, Blackfriars, Bankside, London Bridge, St. Katharine's. London Cycle Network (www.londoncyclenetwork.org.uk) and London Cycling Campaign (www.lcc.org.uk) advise on aspects of biking about town.

TIPS

● London is huge. It may take more than an hour to reach your destination, so allow plenty of time—and plan your day to avoid criss-crossing the city.

● Buy a travelcard, which is valid for the entire transport network. Select the appropriate pass for the areas you will visit. Many people find the Zones 1 and 2 range is adequate; pay a supplement when you go outside it.

● Use common sense when travelling alone at night, but there is no need to be unduly concerned.

● Do not smoke on any public transport—it is banned.

FUN TOURS

There are many quirky ways to see London. Below are four ideas:

● Original London walks
☎ 020 7624 9255;
www.walks.com

● Open House Architecture
☎ 020 7383 2131;
www.londonopenhouse.org

● Cabair Helicopters
☎ 020 8953 4411;
www.cabairhelicopters.com

● By water (▷ 70–71)

NEED TO KNOW GETTING AROUND

Essential Facts

VISA AND TRAVEL INSURANCE

Check visa and passport requirements before travelling, see www.fco.gov.uk or www.britainusa. com. EU citizens are covered for medical expenses with an EHIC card; insurance to cover illness and theft is still strongly advised. Visitors from outside the EU should check their insurance coverage and if necessary, buy a supplementary policy.

MONEY

Try to arrive at the airport or train station with some British coins, or a £10 or £5 note. If you travel to your hotel by Tube, the self-service machines accept money and credit cards.

£5

£10

£20

£50

ELECTRICITY
● Standard supply is 240V. Motor-driven equipment needs a specific frequency; in the UK it is 50 cycles per second (kHz).

EMERGENCY TELEPHONE NUMBERS
● For police, fire or ambulance, ☎ 999 from any telephone, free of charge. The call goes directly to the emergency services. Tell the operator which street you are on and the nearest landmark, intersection or house number; stay by the telephone until help arrives.

MEDICAL TREATMENT
● EU nationals and citizens of some other countries with special arrangements (Australia and New Zealand) may receive free National Health Service (NHS) medical treatment if they have the correct documentation (an EHIC card for EU visitors).
● All other visitors have to pay.
● If you need an ambulance ☎ 999 on any telephone, free of charge or 112 from most mobiles/cellphones.
● NHS hospitals with 24-hour emergency departments include: University College Hospital ✉ Gower Street (entrance in Grafton Way), WC1 ☎ 0845 155 5000; Chelsea and Westminster Hospital ✉ 369 Fulham Road, SW10 ☎ 020 8746 8000.
● Private hospitals, with no emergency unit, include the Cromwell Hospital ✉ Cromwell Road, SW5 ☎ 020 7460 2000.
● Great Chapel Street Medical Centre ✉ 13 Great Chapel Street, W1 ☎ 020 7437 9360 is an NHS clinic open to all, but visitors from countries without the NHS reciprocal agreement must pay.
● NHS Direct: ☎ 0845 4647.
● Dental advice: ☎ 0845 063 1188. Helpline 0870 333 1188 🕐 Mon–Fri 9–5.
● Eye specialist: Moorfields Eye Hospital ✉ City Road, EC1 ☎ 020 7253 3411; Dolland & Aitchison ✉ 233 Regent Street, W1 ☎ 020 7495 8209 (opticians and on-site workshop

for glasses and contact lenses).

● For homeopathic pharmacies, practitioners and advice: the British Homeopathic Association ☎ 08704 443950; www.trusthomeopathy.org

MEDICINES

● Many drugs cannot be bought over the counter. For an NHS prescription, pay a modest flat rate; if a private doctor prescribes, you pay the full cost. To claim charges back on insurance, keep receipts. Chemists that keep longer hours include: Bliss Chemist ✉ 5 Marble Arch, W1 ☎ 020 7723 6116 🕐 Daily 9am–midnight; Ainsworth's Homeopathic Pharmacy ✉ 36 New Cavendish Street ☎ 020 7935 5330 🕐 Mon–Fri 9–5, Sat 9–4.

OPENING HOURS

● Major attractions: seven days a week; some open late certain days of each week.
● Shops: six days a week; some open on Sun and for late-night shopping.
● Banks: Mon–Fri 9.30–5; a few remain later or open on Sat mornings. Bureaux de Change generally have longer opening hours. ATMs are abundant.
● Post offices: usually Mon–Fri 9–5.30, Sat 9–12.30.

PUBLIC HOLIDAYS

● 1 Jan; Good Friday; Easter Mon; May Day (first Mon in May); last Mon in May; last Mon in Aug; 25 Dec; 26 Dec.

NEWSPAPERS AND MAGAZINES

Newspapers include the *Financial Times*, the *Daily Telegraph*, the *Independent*, the *Guardian*, the *Daily Express* and *The Times*, Sunday papers include *Sunday Times*, *Sunday Telegraph*, *Observer* and *Independent on Sunday*. London's only evening paper, the *Evening Standard* (Mon–Fri), first edition out around noon, is strong on entertainment and nightlife (www.thisislondon.co.uk). *Time Out* (published weekly Wed) lists almost everything going (www.timeout.com).

HELP

● Alcoholics Anonymous 0845 769 7555 daily 10am–10pm.
● Narcotics Anonymous 0845 373 3366 daily 10am–10pm.
● Samaritans 08457 909090 24 hours for anyone with an emotional problem.

EMBASSIES	
Australian High Commission	✉ Australia House, Strand, WC2 ☎ 020 7379 4334; www.australia.org.uk
Canadian High Commission	✉ 38 Grosvenor Street, W1 ☎ 020 7258 6600; www.canada.org.uk
New Zealand High Commission	✉ New Zealand House, 80 Haymarket, SW1 ☎ 020 7930 8422; www.nzembassy.com
Embassy of the US	✉ 24 Grosvenor Square, W1 ☎ 020 7499 9000; www.usembassy.org.uk

MAILING A LETTER

Stamps are sold at post offices and some newsagents and shops. Trafalgar Square Post Office stays open late:
✉ William IV Street, WC2
🕐 Mon–Fri 8.30–6.30, Sat 9–5.30. Letter boxes are red.

TELEVISION

Excluding satellite, cable and digital, there are five main national terrestrial channels in Britain: BBC1, BBC2, ITV1, Channel 4 and Channel 5. There is no advertising on the BBC channels, which are funded by a licence fee from all owners of a TV.
Not many homes in Britain have cable, although it is increasing. Digital satellite receivers are free and allow viewers to receive skeleton service of free digital channels. A monthly subscription must be paid to view all sports and film channels. Digital terrestrial television receivers can be purchased with one payment allowing viewers to watch more channels than on normal terrestial services.

STUDENTS

Holders of an International Student Identity Card will be able to obtain some good concessions on travel and entrance fees.

● Almost all attractions and shops close Christmas Day; many close 24 Dec, 1 Jan and Good Fri as well. Some shops, restaurants and attractions remain open throughout, but check.

SENSIBLE PRECAUTIONS

● Do not wear valuables that can be snatched.
● Keep valuables in a hotel or bank safe box.
● Make a note of all passport, ticket and credit card numbers, and keep it in a separate place. Carry photocopies of the key papers of your passport.
● Keep money, passport and credit cards in a fully closed bag. Carry only a small amount of cash and keep it out of sight.
● Keep your bag in sight at all times—do not sling it over your back or put it on the floor of a café, pub or cinema.
● At night, try not to travel alone; if you must, either prebook a taxi (not a mini-cab) or keep to well-lighted streets and use a bus or under-ground train where there are other people.

PHONES

● Check the mark-up rate before making a call from a hotel.
● London numbers (now 8 digits) are prefixed with the code 020 when dialling from outside the city. To call London from abroad, dial the country code 44, then just 20, then the 8 digit number.
● Public phones accept coins, phonecards and credit cards.
● Operator ☎ 100 to check costs, reverse charges, or call another person in the UK via the operator.
● Directory enquiries: there are many options ☎ 0800 953 0720 for details and prices.
● International calls: ☎ 155 for the international operator or to reverse charges.
● To make international calls from the UK, dial 00, then the country code (1 for the US).
● Beware of high charges on numbers prefixed 08 or 09 (0800 is free).
● Before leaving home, consult with your

cell/ mobile phone company on coverage and rates.

TICKETS

● To book rock and pop concerts, London shows and big events, call Globaltickets ☎ 0870 842 2248, www.globaltickets.com; or Ticketmaster ☎ 0870 534 4444, www.ticketmaster.co.uk (who also provide a specialist section for sports events). Beware: check booking fees carefully. Touts outside music and sports venues may offer tickets.

TOURIST INFORMATION

● **Britain information** Britain and London Visitor Centre ✉ 1 Lower Regent Street, south of Piccadilly Circus, SW1; www.visitbritain.com ◐ Daily 8–5. Personal callers only, no phone ⊕ Piccadilly Circus

● **London Information Centres** ✉ Leicester Square, W1 ☎ 020 7437 4370; www.londontown.com ◐ Mon–Fri 8am–6pm, Sat–Sun 10–6 ⊕ Leicester Square
✉ Waterloo International Terminus, SE1 ◐ Daily ⊕ Waterloo

● **Local Centres** For detailed information on the City of London: City of London Information Centre ✉ St. Paul's Churchyard, EC4 ☎ 020 7332 1456; www.cityoflondon.gov.uk Greenwich Tourist Information Centre ✉ 2 Cutty Sark Gardens, Greenwich, SE10 ☎ 020 8858 6376; www.greenwich.gov.uk Richmond Tourist Information Centre ✉ Old Town Hall, Whittaker Avenue, Richmond, Surrey ☎ 020 8940 9125; www.visitrichmond.co.uk

● **Hotel Reservations** Visit London Booking Line: www.visitlondon.com runs a hotel booking service; credit card payment only; £5 fee. Also book in person at London Information Centre (see above) for a small fee.

● The Automobile Association (AA) publishes an annual hotel guide (available from bookshops), the *Hotel Guide*, covering all of Britain with a section on London. For a database of AA inspected hotels see www.theaa.com.

CREDIT CARDS

Credit cards are widely accepted throughout London and Britain; Visa and MasterCard are the most popular, followed by American Express, Diners Club and JCB. Credit cards can also be used for withdrawing currency from cash machines (ATMs) at any bank displaying the appropriate sign.

If your credit cards are lost report each one immediately to the relevant company and the police, also call your bank. To discover your credit card company's local 24-hour emergency number go to www.ukphonebook.co.uk; free but you have to register.

TIPPING

10 per cent for restaurants, taxis, hairdressers and other services is acceptable, although good service can be rewarded with up to 15 per cent. Inspect restaurant bills to see if a service charge has already been added or is included. No tipping in theatres, cinemas, concert halls or in pubs and bars (unless there is waitress service).

Timeline

EARLY LONDON

Emperor Claudius invades Britain in AD43; a deep-water port, Londinium, is soon established.

In the year 200 the Romans put a wall around Londinium, now capital of Britannia Superior; they withdraw in 410.

THE GREAT FIRE

The fire broke out at a baker's near Pudding Lane on the night of 2 September 1666. Raging for four days and nights, it destroyed four-fifths of the City of London and 13,200 homes. Sir Christopher Wren became the grand architect of the consequent rebuilding of London.

1042 Edward the Confessor becomes king making London capital of England and Westminster his home; builds the abbey church of St. Peter.

1066 The Norman king, William the Conqueror, defeats King Harold at the Battle of Hastings; begins the Tower of London.

1485 Tudor rule commences, ending in 1603 with the death of Elizabeth I.

1533 Henry VIII breaks with Rome to marry Anne Boleyn; establishes the Church of England.

1649 Charles I is executed in Whitehall; the Commonwealth (1649–53) and Protectorate (1653–59) govern England until Charles II is restored to the throne in 1660.

1666 The Great Fire of London.

1759 The British Museum, London's first public museum opens.

1851 The Great Exhibition is held in Hyde Park.

1863 World's first urban underground train service opens. In 1890 the first deep-dug train runs (known as 'the Tube').

1939–45 Blitz bombings destroy a third of the City of London and much of the docks.

124

1951 Festival of Britain held on the site of the South Bank arts complex.

1960s The Beatles, Carnaby Street and the King's Road help create 'swinging London'.

1981 Revival of Docklands begins.

1994 First Eurostar trains link London and Paris through Channel Tunnel.

1999 Londoners elect their first mayor of all London, Ken Livingstone.

2000 Major millennium projects are completed, rejuvenating central London.

2002 Queen Elizabeth II celebrates her Golden Jubilee. City Hall completed for the Mayor of London.

2003 Clarence House, formerly the Queen Mother's home, opens to the public. Fiftieth anniversary of Queen Elizabeth II's accession to the throne.

2005 London wins the vote to hold the Olympic Games in 2012 and begins preparations.

2007 Eurostar trains use refurbished St. Pancras Station, no longer Waterloo.

2008 Boris Johnson ousts Ken Livingstone, voted by Londoners to be the new Mayor and bringing a new agenda of plans for the city.

GROWING CITY

During the 16th century, London was Europe's fastest-growing city; its population rose from 75,000 to 200,000.

By 1700, London was Europe's biggest and wealthiest city, with about 700,000 people.

London continued to grow, from under 1 million in 1800 to 6.5 million by 1900, peaking in the 1930s and 1940s at 10 million.

The population is now 7.5 million but rising.

Oliver Cromwell (far left). A mural depicts a scene from the Great Fire of London (middle left). Cromwell expelling the Parliament, 1653 (middle right). City Hall—headquarters of the Mayor of London and the Greater London Authority (right)

Index

A

accommodation 107–112
  bed-and-breakfast 108
  hostels 108
  hotels 17, 108, 109–112
  reservations 108, 115, 123
airports 116–117
Albert Memorial 89
All-Hallows-by-the-Tower 40
Apsley House (Wellington Museum) 74
art and antiques 12, 18, 54, 77, 90, 104
auction houses 54, 55, 77

B

Bank of England Museum 40
banks 121
Banqueting House 8, 64
bed-and-breakfast 108
Benjamin Franlin House 74
Big Ben 65
biking 119
boat commuter services 119
bookshops 12, 54, 55, 77, 104
Borough Market 27
British Library 99
British Museum 8, 48–49
Brompton Oratory 89
Buckingham Palace 8, 62–63
Burghers of Calais 74
Burlington Arcade 11
buses 118

C

Cabinet War Rooms 74
Canary Wharf 99
Channel Tunnel 117
Charles I statue 74
Chelsea Physic Garden 99
chemists 121
children's entertainment 18
Chiswick House 99
Christchurch Spitalfields 40
cinemas 31, 79, 91
City Hall 4, 27
Clarence House 74
Cleopatra's Needle 52
climate and seasons 114
Clockmaker's Museum 40
clubs see entertainment and nightlife
coach travel 117
comedy venues 79
concert venues 13, 31, 43, 56, 79, 91
County Hall 27
Courtauld Gallery 51
Covent Garden Piazza 52

Covent Garden to Bloomsbury 45–58
  entertainment and nightlife 56
  map 46–7
  restaurants 57–58
  shopping 54–55
  sights 48–53
credit cards 123
Cutty Sark 103

D

Dali Universe 27
dental services 120
department stores 12, 104
Design Museum 27
Dickens' House 52
disabilities, visitors with 118
Dr. Johnson's House 40
dress code 14
driving 118
Dulwich Picture Gallery 99

E

eating out 14–15, 16
  see also restaurants
electricity 120
embassies 121
emergency telephone numbers 120
entertainment and nightlife 13, 17
  Covent Garden to Bloomsbury 56
  Fleet Street to the Tower 43
  Hyde Park and around 91
  London farther afield 105
  South Bank 31
  Westminster and St. James 79
Eros 52
events and festivals 114
excursions 102

F

fashion shopping 12, 54, 55, 85, 90, 104
ferry services 117
Firepower Museum 100
Fleet Street to the Tower 33–44
  entertainment and nightlife 43
  map 34–35
  restaurants 44
  shopping 43
  sights 36–41
  walk 42
food and drink
  eating out 14–15, 16

  shopping for 12, 54, 55, 77, 90
  see also restaurants
Foundling Museum 52

G

gifts and souvenirs 10–11
Gipsy Moth IV 103
Golden Hinde 27
Green Park 74
Greenwich 9, 96, 103
Guildhall Art Gallery 40

H

Ham House 100
Hampstead Heath 100
Hampton Court Palace 102
Handel House Museum 52
Harrods 85, 90
Harvey Nichols 85, 90
Hayward Gallery 27
helplines 121
history 124–125
HMS Belfast 27
Holy Trinity, Sloane Square 89
homeopathy 121
hostels 108
hotels 17, 108, 109–112
Houses of Parliament 9, 65
Hunterian Museum 52–53
Hyde Park 89
Hyde Park and around 81–92
  entertainment and nightlife 91
  map 82–83
  restaurants 92
  shopping 90
  sights 84–89

I

Imperial War Museum 28
linsurance 120
Internet access 115
itineraries 6–7

J

jazz venues 56, 105
Jewish Museum 100

K

Kensington Palace and Gardens 9, 84
Kenwood House 100
Knightsbridge shopping spree 9, 85

L

London Aquarium 28
London Bridge 42, 71
London Eye 9, 24–25
London farther afield 93–106

entertainment and nightlife 105
excursions 102
map 94–95
restaurants 106
shopping 104
sights 96–102
walk 103
London Pass 115, 119
London Transport Museum 53
London Wetland Centre 101
London Zoo 101
lost/stolen property 117, 123

M
Madame Tussaud's 101
maps
  Covent Garden to
    Bloomsbury 46–47
  Fleet Street to the Tower
    34–35
  Hyde Park and around
    82–83
  London farther afield
    94–95
  South Bank 22–23
  Westminster and St.
    James's 60–61
markets 12, 27, 43, 97, 104
medical treatment 120–121
medicines 121
money 120
Museum in Docklands 101
Museum of London 9, 36

N
National Gallery 8, 66
National Maritime Museum
  100, 103
National Portrait Gallery 8, 67
Natural History Museum 8, 86
Nelson's Column 75
newspapers and magazines
  121

O
Old Royal Naval College 103
Oliver Cromwell statue 75
opening hours 121, 122
opera 56, 91
opticians 120–121

P
passports and visas 117, 120
Percival David Foundation of
  Chinese Art 53
Peter Pan statue 89
Petrie Museum 53
Petticoat Lane 43
phones 122–123

Photographers' Gallery 53
Portobello Road Market 8, 97
post offices and postal
  services 121, 122
public holidays 121
public transport 115, 118–119
pubs and bars 12, 14, 105

Q
Queen Alexandra Memorial 75
Queen's Gallery 63

R
Regent's Park 101
restaurants 15, 16
  Covent Garden to
    Bloomsbury 57–58
  Fleet Street to the Tower 44
  Hyde Park and around 92
  London farther afield 106
  South Bank 32
  Westminster and St.
    James 80
Royal Academy of Arts 53
Royal Albert Hall 91
Royal Botanic Gardens, Kew
  8, 98
Royal Festival Hall 29, 31
Royal Mews 63
Russell Square 53

S
safety, personal 122
St. Bartholomew-the-Great 41
St. James's Park 8, 68
St. James's, Piccadilly 75
St. Margaret, Lothbury 41
St. Paul's Cathedral 8, 37
Science Museum 8, 87
Shakespeare's Globe 31, 91
shopping 10–12, 16, 18, 121
  Covent Garden to
    Bloomsbury 54–55
  Fleet Street to the Tower 43
  Hyde Park and around 90
  London farther afield 104
  Westminster and St.
    James's 77
sightseeing tours 119
Sir John Soane's Museum
  8, 50
smoking etiquette 119
Somerset House 8, 51
South Bank 13, 20–32
  entertainment and
    nightlife 31
  map 22–23
  restaurants 32
  sights 24–28
  walk 29

Southwark Cathedral 28, 29
Spencer House 75
sports venues 105
student travellers 122

T
Tate Britain 8, 69
Tate Modern 8, 26
taxis 116, 117, 118
television 122
Temple Church 41
Temple of Mithras 41
Thames Flood Barrier 71
Thames river cruise 8, 70–71
theatres 31, 43, 56, 79, 91, 115
30 St. Mary Axe ('Gherkin') 41
ticket outlets 79, 123
time differences 114
tipping 57, 123
tourist information 115, 123
Tower Bridge 29, 71
Tower of London 9, 38–39
train services 116
travel arrangements 116–117
travel passes 119

U
Underground (Tube) 118

V
V & A Museum of Childhood
  101
Victoria and Albert Museum
  9, 88
Vinopolis 28

W
walks
  around the City 42
  Greenwich 103
  South Bank 29
  Westminster and St.
    James's 76
Wallace Collection 89
websites 115
Westminster Abbey 9, 72–73
Westminster and St. James's
  59–80
  entertainment and nightlife
    79
  map 60–61
  restaurants 80
  shopping 77
  sights 62–75
  walk 76
Whitechapel Art Gallery 101
Windsor and Windsor
  Castle 102
Winston Churchill's Britain
  at War Experience 28

London's
25 BEST

WRITTEN BY Louise Nicholson
DESIGN WORK Jacqueline Bailey
COVER DESIGN Tigist Getachew
INDEXER Marie Lorimer
IMAGE RETOUCHING AND REPRO Michael Moody, Sarah Montgomery
REVIEWING EDITOR Paul Eisenberg
EDITORIAL MANAGEMENT Apostrophe S Limited
SERIES EDITOR Marie-Claire Jefferies
UPDATED BY Robin Barton

© AA Media Limited 2009 (registered office: Fanum House, Basing View, Basingstoke, Hampshire RG21 4EA, registered number 06112600).

All rights reserved. Published in the United States by Fodor's Travel, a division of Random House, Inc., and simultaneously in Canada by Random House of Canada Limited, Toronto. Distributed by Random House, Inc., New York. No maps, illustrations, or other portions of this book may be reproduced in any form without written permission from the publishers.

Fodor's is a registered trademark of Random House, Inc.
Published in the United Kingdom by AA Publishing

ISBN 978-1-4000-0792-9

EIGHTH EDITION

IMPORTANT TIP
Time inevitably brings changes, so always confirm prices, travel facts, and other perishable information when it matters. Although Fodor's cannot accept responsibility for errors, you can use this guide in the confidence that we have taken every care to ensure its accuracy.

SPECIAL SALES
This book is available for special discounts for bulk purchases for sales promotions or premiums. Special editions, including personalized covers, excerpts of existing books, and corporate imprints, can be created in large quantities for special needs. For more information, write to Special Markets/Premium Sales, 1745 Broadway, MD 6–2, New York, NY 10019 or email specialmarkets@randomhouse.com.

Color separation by Keenes, Andover, UK
Printed and bound by Leo Paper Products, China
10 9 8 7 6 5

A04659

Enabled by Ordnance Survey® This product includes mapping data licensed from Ordnance Survey® with the permission of the Controller of Her Majesty's Stationery Office. © Crown copyright 2011. All rights reserved. Licence number 100021153

The Automobile Association wishes to thank the following photographers, companies and picture libraries for their assistance in the preparation of this book.

Abbreviations for the picture credits are as follows – (t) top; (b) bottom; (l) left; (r) right; (c) centre; (AA) AA World Travel Library

1 AA/M Jourdan; 2 AA/R Ireland; 3 AA/R Ireland; 4t AA/R Ireland; 4c AA/W Voysey; 5t AA/R Ireland; 5b AA/M Jourdan; 6t AA/R Ireland; 6cl AA/B Smith; 6c AA/P Wilson; 6cr AA/P Wilson; 6bl AA/G Wrona; 6bc AA/J McMillan; 6br AA/J McMillan; 7t AA/R Ireland; 7cl AA/M Trelawney; 7cr AA/R Strange; 7bl AA/S McBride; 7bc AA/S McBride; 7br AA/R Strange; 8 AA/R Ireland; 9 AA/R Ireland; 10t AA/R Ireland; 10/11 AA/J A Tims; 10ct AA/M Jourdan; 10cb AA/M Trelawney; 10b AA/M Jourdan; 11t AA/R Ireland; 11ct AA/R Strange; 11cb AA/C Sawyer; 11b AA/M Jourdan; 12 AA/R Ireland; 13t AA/R Ireland; 13ctt AA/M Jourdan; 13ct AA/M Jourdan; 13c AA; 13cb Brand X Pictures; 13b AA/P Wilson; 14t AA/R Ireland; 14ctt AA/M Jourdan; 14ct AA/C Sawyer; 14cb AA/M Jourdan; 14b AA; 15 AA/R Ireland; 16r AA/R Ireland; 16ct AA/M Trelawney; 16cb AA/P Kenward; 16b AA/C Sawyer; 17t AA/R Ireland; 17tc AA/C Sawyer; 17ct Photodisc; 17cb Digital Vision; 17b AA/M Jourdan; 18t AA/R Ireland; 18tc AA/M Jourdan; 18ct AA/S McBride; 18cb AA/J A Tims; 18b AA/M Jourdan; 19t AA/M Jourdan; 19ctt AA/S McBride; 19ct AA/M Jourdan; 19cb AA/J McMillan; 19cbb AA/M Jourdan; 19b AA/C Sawyer; 20/21 AA/C Sawyer; 24/25 AA/R Ireland; 25 AA/M Jourdan; 26l AA/M Jourdan; 26bc AA/M Jourdan; 26r AA/M Jourdan; 27t AA/C Sawyer; 27bl AA/S McBride; 27br AA/S McBride; 28t AA/C Sawyer; 28b AA/S McBride; 29 AA/R Victor; 30 AA/R Turpin; 31 AA/P Kenward; 31b AA/P Kenward; 32 AA/M Jourdan; 33 AA/P Kenward; 36l AA/S McBride; 36r AA/T Woodcock; 37l AA/R Strange; 37c Sampson Lloyd/St Paul's Cathedral; 37r Sampson Lloyd/St Paul's Cathedral; 38l AA/R Mort; 38/39t AA/S McBride; 38/39b AA/S McBride; 39t AA/W Voysey; 39b AA/S McBride; 40t AA/C Sawyer; 40bl Bank of England Museum; 40br AA/P Kenward; 41 AA/C Sawyer; 41bl AA/R Turpin; 41br AA/P Kenward; 42 AA/R Victor; 43t AA/R Strange; 43c Digital Vision; 44 AA/C Sawyer; 45 AA/M Trelawney; 48 British Museum; 48/49 British Museum; 50l AA/J A Tims; 50r AA/J A Tims; 51l AA/J A Tims; 51r AA/M Jourdan; 52t AA/C Sawyer; 52bl AA/P Baker; 52br Handel House Museum; 53t AA/C Sawyer; 53bl AA/M Jourdan; 53br AA/P Kenward; 54 AA/M Chaplow; 55 AA/P Kenward; 56 AA/P Kenward; 57 AA/T Harris; 58 AA/C Sawyer; 59 AA/R Strange; 62 AA/T Woodcock; 62/63t AA/S McBride; 62/63b AA/J McMillan; 63c AA/S McBride; 63cr AA/M Jourdan; 64 AA/J A Tims; 65 AA/W Voysey; 66l AA/J McMillan; 66r AA/J A Tims; 67l National Portrait Gallery © Andrew Putler; 67r National Portrait Gallery © Andrew Putler; 68l AA/R Victor; 68r AA/J A Tims; 69 AA/T Woodcock; 70 AA; 71t AA/R Strange; 71cl AA/C Sawyer; 71cr AA/W Voysey; 72 AA/J A Tims; 72/73t AA/J A Tims; 72/73b AA/R Strange; 73 AA/J A Tims; 74t AA/C Sawyer; 74bl AA/W Voysey; 74br AA/T Woodcock; 75t AA/C Sawyer; 75bl AA/P Kenward; 75br AA/J McMillan; 76 AA/R Victor; 77 AA/P Kenward; 78 AA/R Mort; 79 AA/P Wilson; 80 AA/C Sawyer; 81 AA/B Smith; 84l AA/M Jourdan; 84c AA/R Strange; 84r AA/R Strange; 85l AA/P Kenward; 85r AA/T Woodcock; 86l AA/M Jourdan; 86r AA/M Jourdan; 87l Science Museum; 87r Science Museum; 88 AA/P Kenward; 89t AA/C Sawyer; 89bl AA/N Sumner; 89br AA; 90 AA; 91 Digital Vision; 92 AA/C Sawyer; 93 AA/M Jourdan; 96l AA/N Setchfield; 96r AA/N Setchfield; 97l AA/M Jourdan; 97r AA/M Jourdan; 98l AA/R Mort; 98r AA/W Voysey; 99t AA/C Sawyer; 99bl AA/R Mort; 99br AA/J A Tims; 100t AA/C Sawyer; 100bl AA/M Trelawney; 100br AA/G Wrona; 101t AA/C Sawyer; 101b AA/J A Tims; 102t AA/R Turpin; 102cl AA/R Mort; 102c AA/R Turpin; 102cr AA/R Mort; 102bl AA/J Miller; 102bc AA/C Jones; 102br AA/W Voysey; 103 AA/R Victor; 104 AA/K Paterson; 105t Digital Vision; 105b Photodisc; 106 AA/C Sawyer; 107 AA/W Voysey; 108t AA/C Sawyer; 108ct AA/R Strange; 108c AA/P Wilson; 108cb AA/S McBride; 108b AA; 109 AA/C Sawyer; 110 AA/C Sawyer; 111 AA/C Sawyer; 112 AA/C Sawyer; 113 AA/C Sawyer; 114 AA/M Jourdan; 115 AA/M Jourdan; 116 AA/M Jourdan; 117 AA/M Jourdan; 118 AA/M Jourdan; 119 AA/M Jourdan; 120t AA/M Jourdan; 120b MRI Bankers' Guide to Foreign Currency, Houston, USA; 121 AA/M Jourdan; 122 AA/M Jourdan; 123 AA/M Jourdan; 124t AA/M Jourdan; 124bl AA; 124br AA/R Strange; 125t AA/M Jourdan; 125bl AA; 125br AA/N Setchfield

Every effort has been made to trace the copyright holders, and we apologise in advance for an unintentional omissions or errors. We would be please to apply any corrections to any following edition of this publication.